Empowering Themselves

# A
# FINANCIAL
# SURVIVAL
# GUIDE

*For Women at Risk of Drowning Financially
Before, During and After Divorce*

**Antoinette Babek, CPFC, AFC
and
Hollis Colquhoun, Financial Advisor, CPFC, AFC**

This edition published by
Dog Ear Publishing
4010 W. 86th Street, Ste H
Indianapolis, IN 46268

www.dogearpublishing.net

ISBN: 978-159858-981-8
This book is printed on acid-free paper.

Printed in the United States of America

# Contents

iii

# Contents

# Introduction

We were two women going down parallel paths, Antoinette was married for thirty years and had three sons; Hollis was married for twenty with three daughters. Our paths converged at a nonprofit credit counseling agency where we became very concerned about our female clients' lack of financial education and wanted to do something about it. As a result, we have written this guide to give basic information and resources to help women become more financially aware and independent.

This book should be used as a financial companion, to help you track your spending, construct your budget, understand your worth, chart your progress, and achieve your financial goals. Included are some of our personal experiences as well as special alerts to reinforce important topics and potential financial hazards. Not only do we want you to financially survive but ultimately we want you to become captain of your financial ship, the commander of your financial destiny.

# About the Authors

Antoinette Babek started her career path at hairdresser school, got married at the age of 20, then became partners with her husband and built a successful tire distribution business. In-between raising a family, she took classes in marketing and sales part-time, and helped steer her company in new and creative directions. While her husband was in charge of sales, Antoinette managed the finances, marketing, and advertising. After the divorce, she studied and got her certification as a consulting hypnotist. In 2007, Antoinette became an Accredited Financial Counselor and over the last two years has counseled thousands of clients throughout the country.

Hollis Colquhoun earned a BA in Economics and went straight to Wall Street, where she became an institutional salesperson and registered representative for several New York City brokerage firms. After 20 years in the financial industry, she retired to spend more time with her children, devoting most of her spare time helping local charitable organizations. After her divorce, Hollis wanted to combine her financial background and nonprofit experience, so she became an Accredited Financial Counselor for a nonprofit credit counseling agency. She has given workshops on personal money management for nonprofit groups and New Jersey State welfare-to-work programs and has also counseled thousands of clients while at the agency. In 2008, Hollis became a registered Financial Advisor for Waddell and Reed Financial Advisors.

# Financial Empowerment

According to ancient philosophy, there are four powerful elements in the universe: earth, wind, fire and air. There are also four human sources of power that energize our society: the body, mind, spirit, and *money.* To realize the power of the body, it has to be cared for and handled properly. To optimize the power of the mind, it has to be used wisely and allowed to grow. With the spirit, in order to understand its essence, it must be contemplated and nurtured. That leaves money. To maximize its power, money has to be contemplated, handled properly, and allowed to grow. These human power sources must be fed and harnessed for you to survive and ultimately succeed in today's society.

This guide will concentrate on one power source: money. It will teach you how to understand and use money wisely, and how to make it work for you, whether you're in a relationship, married or alone. Being aware and grabbing hold of money's financial power will ultimately empower you.

Money is such an elemental aspect of life and yet so intertwined with emotion and ego. Almost all of the female clients we have counseled admit they feel uncomfortable or have problems talking to their partner, fiancé, or spouse about money. When a relationship is strained, it is normal for financial issues to become hypersensitive topics. Obviously, having an open and honest financial dialogue is best, but if such communication hasn't been the norm throughout your relationship, it is pretty impossible to cultivate when everything else is turning sour.

Financial awareness and good money management skills are key components for building a successful life alone or with a partner. You cannot survive if you avoid the topic of money or remain clueless about your finances. Whatever happens in your marriage or relationship or life, you must take the steps necessary to be in control of your financial destiny.

Being in control of your financial destiny is important because:

1. Your financial health is as necessary to your survival as your physical and mental health.
2. Financial awareness and planning in the present will bring you more financial security in the future.
3. If *you* are not financially in control, then someone else is, and their interests might not be in your best interest.

The following pages will provide the basic education and survival skills you will need to take financial control of your life. Don't be afraid if some of the terms are hard to understand. Keep reading, fill in the charts and utilize the resources in the back of the guide. If you gather the necessary financial information and follow the steps, you will acquire the understanding and means to financially empower yourself.

# PART I

# Married Women Empowering Themselves Financially

*"Where did my husband go, and how long can I tread water?"*

# I

# Married Women Empowering Themselves Financially

When you get married, you assume that your marriage will last forever. In the beginning, you and your husband start to form a spiritual as well as an economic partnership. You both probably work full-time and since you are living together, your incomes and expenses quickly become interconnected, whether or not you have created a financial plan. After a few years, you may start a family, and, in order to take care of the children and household, you may cut your hours to part-time or stop working entirely. Your new job as mother and household manager ends up being more than full-time, in reality 24/7; unfortunately it's a non-paying job. Because you are no longer bringing home a paycheck, your sense of financial strength or worth may shrink, particularly if you and your husband do not have an ongoing financial dialogue or formal plan.

In your relationship, you and your husband are each performing essential economic tasks to keep the household running smoothly, but it is the breadwinner, the *money maker*—usually the husband—who becomes the financial decision-maker. As the relationship evolves, a wife's self-worth and economic support may be determined by her husband, unless she is financially well informed. Should the relationship fall apart, and approximately 50% do, the financially uninformed woman must prepare and be willing and able to fight for her financial rights. Consider the following:

*"On average, a woman spends more of her adult life unmarried than married, and nine out of ten women will be solely responsible for their finances at some point in their lives."* [1]

> *Antoinette's Experience:* **My husband and I were married for 30 years and had our own business. For the majority of that time, I took only enough income to save the maximum allowed for my IRA contribution, and throughout our marriage, I allowed my husband to pay himself the lion's share of the income. I wasn't really concerned because I felt we were partners—husband and wife—so we shared the income. But I realized when we split up and closed the business that I had paid very little into Social Security and had no savings of my own.** *If you are working with your husband in your own business, make sure you take care of yourself financially; pay yourself and have emergency savings.*

It is crucial that all women have a basic financial education to ensure their financial survival and well-being in the present and future. Just as you need to take good care of your physical health by developing good eating and exercise habits and having regular checkups, you must take care of your financial health by developing good budgetary habits and performing monthly financial checkups.

4

The first step to being financially prepared while you are married or in a relationship is to gather the information that will answer this crucial question:

## WHAT AM I WORTH?

To help you organize and categorize this financial information, we will help you put together 5 folders that will lead to the answer:

1. "Monetary Assets"
2. "IRS Annual Tax Returns"
3. "Investment Assets"
4. "Tangible Assets"
5. "Liabilities"

Your worth is divided into two parts: your **earning power** and your **net worth**. Earning power is the ability to create income. Net worth is the value of your property, investments and monetary accounts (assets) minus your debts or liabilities.

## YOUR EARNING POWER

How do you determine your earning power?
Earning power in a marriage consists of:

1. Income earned through employment, Social Security benefits
2. Savings achieved through cutting costs, freeing up income
3. Potential future earnings and retirement income

## Earned Income:

While you are married and working outside the home, your income is usually combined with your husband's to create the household income. Your current earning power is your income minus your husband's. It is easy to track household income (yours/his/combined) by reviewing financial records. Bank account statements arrive every month. Be sure to open both your individual and joint statements, read them and understand what they are reporting. Today, most employers are using automatic payroll deposits, so you should be able to identify the money coming in on a regular basis. Because more and more business and banking statements are in paperless form online, you also need to be aware of all online accounts.

Download and print the statements or call and ask the bank or financial institution for a monthly statement to keep for your records.

Checklist for "Monetary Asset" Accounts Showing Earned Income:

"Monetary Assets" Folder:

    _Bank Checking Account (Joint)
    _Bank Checking Account (Yours)
    _Bank Checking Account (His)
    _Credit Union Accounts
    _Regular Savings Account (Joint)
    _Regular Savings Account (Individual)

Put these statements into the folder marked "**Monetary Assets**." Employment income will usually be deposited in either checking or savings accounts. There are other monetary accounts that don't have to do with earned income directly, such as special purpose savings accounts, CD's (certificates of deposit) and savings bonds, that should also be placed in the **"Monetary Assets"** folder. All of the accounts in this folder are known as your **liquid** or **monetary** assets because they can easily be converted to money or cash.

Gather your annual joint (or individual) IRS tax returns for the last five years and place them in a separate **"Tax Return"** folder.

You may find additional statements that contain financial information regarding assets such as retirement and insurance account statements, titles, deeds, etc. Separate these statements into two more folders: **"Investment Assets,"** e.g., mutual funds, IRA's, whole life insurance (cash value), annuity accounts, and **"Tangible Assets"** or property, e.g., deeds, car titles, jewelry and antique appraisals. The fifth folder labeled **"Liabilities"** or debts, (everything seems to have two names) will be for loan, mortgage, credit card statements, etc. We will address these three other folders later when we look at your net worth.

You and your husband may have your own business. The business profit will be harder to track, but you are probably using an accountant to maintain the company books for tax purposes. By subtracting the monthly business overhead expenses from the total monthly business revenue, the accountant can give you an idea of the approximate net revenue figure.

Ideally, you and your husband are paying yourselves a weekly or monthly salary, and deducting income taxes and Social Security. Often we speak to clients who have their own business but do not pay themselves on a consistent basis; they take money out of the business bank account when it is there. However, this system does not give you an idea of what the company profit is or what your personal earnings are.

You need to calculate and keep track of two figures on a monthly basis: the net business income or revenue after subtracting basic business overhead expenses, and your salary plus any personal expenses that the business pays.

The following are examples of both calculations, assuming you own a retail store:

Business Income Minus Basic Overhead Expenses:

| | |
|---|---|
| September Business Revenue | $5,000 |

| Operating Expenses: | |
|---|---|
| Cost of Goods/Inventory | 2,000 |
| Store Rent | 1,000 |
| Store Utilities | 250 |
| Store Computer/Fax/Phone | 100 |
| Advertising | 50 |
| Net Revenue | $1,600 |

| Personal Expenses Paid by the Business: | |
|---|---|
| SUV Lease Payment | $ 500 |
| Car Insurance | 200 |
| Gasoline | 100 |
| Cell Phone | 100 |

| | |
|---|---|
| Amount Remaining for Owner Salary | $ 700 |

On the top line, it appears that the business is making a decent amount of monthly revenue; however, once the overhead and inventory expenses are subtracted, the net income is drastically reduced. Then, after taking out the personal expenses, which are also partially business-related, the amount left for a salary is minimal. This exercise lets you see what the business is paying for and what you truly have available to pay in salary. If the business is paying for household expenses or you are using a business credit card to pay, when you try to construct a monthly budget matching household income against household expenses using your personal bank or credit card statements, you might forget to include what you charge on the business card or what flows through the company's books.

As you create your personal/household budget, the $700 salary from the above example would be placed in the income category. In addition, the $900 that the business pays for the SUV expenses and the cell phone would also be added to your compensation, because the business is paying these expenses for you. So that you are aware of all of your monthly household costs, the SUV payment, insurance, gasoline and cell phone expenses should be listed in your household budget. In the event your employment situation changes or the business closes, you will have a monthly budget that contains a complete list of your personal expenses.

> *CAUTION*: **Some "business expenses" overlap "household expenses." These costs may be taken as business deductions for tax purposes, but may distort your household budget figures if they aren't included as personal expenses.** *Keep your business budget separate from your household budget when trying to balance your household income and expenses.*

Your household budget will then give you a realistic idea of your real income from the business and all of your true household expenses. As a business owner you will have a clearer understanding of what the business is making, what it can afford to pay you, and what it *is* paying you. You will also have a better indicator of what your household is really spending.

While going through statements and ledgers, you may have difficulty deciphering the language or math. Ask your accountant to go over it with you or go to your bank and ask a representative to help you. Don't be embarrassed if you don't know or understand something. Women who want to financially empower themselves will find out answers; they won't want to remain in the dark.

Keep copies of all monthly, quarterly and yearly financial statements and information in your folders and in a safe place. If your husband has separate accounts but you can't find any written records, check your annual tax return. All of your combined statements and information should be listed on or with your joint IRS return.

Income through employment can consist of the following:

- Take-home salary
- Tips
- Bonuses
- Commissions

Salary or take-home pay will appear on monthly bank statements, but if your husband gets a bonus or commission that is paid out quarterly, semiannually or annually, and you can't quantify this additional income, you will find a yearly income summary either on an IRS W-2 Form, which every employer is required to provide employees by January 31$^{st}$ following the tax year, or on your annual joint tax return.

You or your husband's job may be seasonal, making income fluctuate each month. If this is your situation, take last year's income from your IRS return and divide it by 12 to calculate an average monthly income.

You may also receive income that is not earned income:

- Social Security benefits
- Income from a sale of assets
- Interest and dividends from investments
- Rental income
- Tax refund
- Monetary gifts

If you have overpaid your payroll income taxes throughout the year and anticipate a tax refund, this refund will add to your disposable income, the income you have available to spend. If you sell an asset and receive money, or have investments that pay interest or dividends, this will also increase your overall household income, but be sure to subtract any taxes that might be owed on this income at year-end.

In the following chart, list all of the current monthly household income sources you were able to identify from the bank statements (salary, commissions, bonuses, tips), rental income statements, asset sale documents, investment accounts (interest and dividends), monetary gifts and tax refunds. If your earned income fluctuates dramatically month to month, use an average over the last 12 months.

11

## Average Monthly Household Income

| Income Source | Amount |
|---|---|
| Average After-Tax Salary | |
| Bonus | |
| Commission | |
| Tips | |
| Social Security Benefits | |
| Income from Asset Sale | |
| Interest and Dividends | |
| Rental Income | |
| Monetary Gifts | |
| Tax Refund | |
| Business Contributions | |
| **TOTAL COMBINED INCOME (After-tax)** | |

# ADDING TO SAVINGS, FREEING UP INCOME:

Even if you don't have a paying job, understand that you still have part ownership of the household income. Just because your husband is the money maker, that money is not solely his to control. As we said earlier, you and your husband have built an economic partnership and in many cases have raised a family together. He wouldn't be able to work full-time, take care of the children and manage the household all on his own without creating

12

more expenses, so you make an economic contribution to the marriage by performing tasks that don't *cost* the household anything. You *create* income, not only by performing tasks he'd have to pay for, but by freeing up money to pay for other expenses or to put into savings. Your combined household income, even if you don't have a job for pay, is an important part of *your* personal income calculation and worth. To illustrate this value, make a list of the tasks you perform regularly that result in monthly cost savings for the household:

| JOB | AVERAGE OUTSIDE COST (Monthly) | |
|---|---|---|
| | **Example** | **Yours** |
| Transportation | 100 | |
| Housekeeping | 200 | |
| Cooking | 400 | |
| Laundry | 200 | |
| Tutoring | 100 | |
| Elder Parent Care | 200 | |
| Other | | |
| **TOTAL (After-tax dollars)** | **$2000** | |

Using these sample figures, in order to have the $2,000 per month to pay someone to do these tasks, you would have to earn approximately $2,500 per month before taxes. In this case your efforts would result in cost savings equivalent to earning $30,000 per year. You can make your own chart and add tasks to calculate your monthly cost savings contribution. Even if you don't have a paying full-time job, you provide *real* economic value to the household by lowering expenses, and therefore have *real* personal economic worth in the relationship. You need to recognize and embrace this value.

Be advised that any individual who earns income can participate in an individual retirement account (IRA) and contribute up to $5,000 annually, *and* that any husband (or wife) who is eligible to set up an IRA can also create a spousal IRA for a *non wage-earning spouse* up to the same amount. If you are over 50 years old, you can contribute up to an additional $1,000 per year. Speak to your husband about setting up an IRA for you, if he hasn't already.

## FUTURE INCOME:

Why is it important to focus on future income? Thinking about your future income helps in your financial awareness, preparation and planning. Future income is an estimate, but it is also a component of your worth. Employment, income levels, budgets, and expenses are not static amounts; they are always changing. So are relationships. Having an educated idea of your potential earning power will prepare you for changes in your situation.What would or could your personal income be if your husband lost his job or you were suddenly out on your own? If you have a full-time job, use your current salary, but at the same time get up-to-date information about the employment opportunities in your field. Find out what other companies are paying for comparable work. It may be possible to earn more by changing employers or locations. If you had a career in the past and left for a few years, look into the feasibility of jumping back in. Could you go back to work for your previous employer? Would you need additional training or re-licensing to get up to speed? How much would that process cost and how long would it take? Do some homework to determine what you could realistically earn. Check major online job search sites. If you've never had a full-time job, perhaps you have skills or experience that could generate income or make you a good job candidate. Do you have any special interests or hobbies that could be turned into a profitable, home-based business?

You may have a skill or talent that you think could be turned into a money-making business from home. Be aware that starting and managing your own business is a huge undertaking. While considering this option, it is a good idea to talk to entrepreneurs who are experienced in that business to find out what the startup and ongoing costs would be. Consider becoming an apprentice to an expert or an employee for a company that is in your desired field before venturing out on your own. You would get a more realistic understanding of the market, costs, customer-base and competition, and what it would take to make the business profitable. You would also have less risk and hopefully a more steady paycheck.

*Antoinette's Experience:* **After my divorce, I followed my passion for helping others by becoming a certified consulting hypnotist. I wanted to open my own practice, so when a small space became available in a psychiatrist's office, I rented it. A normal fee for an hypnosis consulting session was $75. so I assumed I would be able to generate a good monthly income. However, after six months I hadn't made enough money to cover the rent and pay myself a salary. My client base wasn't big enough. I moved out of the office and operated the business from my home. If I had written a business plan and investigated the market before I started, I wouldn't have rented the office space.** *When starting a business, first do your research, then create a business plan and find out if it's possible to make enough profit to pay yourself an adequate salary.*

To give you more insight into the costs and benefits of starting a new business, check out the website: **SCORE.org**, run by the Service Corps of Retired Executives. It is a resource site for self-employed business owners, created and overseen by former executives from many professions, offering advice, information, resources and other useful links and blogs. If you do create a business plan that requires a start-up loan, first go to the Small Business Administration website: **SBA.gov**, for loan and resource information.

We have counseled many clients who decided to start their own businesses either during their marriage or after a divorce, but few were able to survive financially because they didn't do enough research. Usually, they would use loans and credit cards to pay for business and personal expenses during the first few years, hoping that their revenues would improve. Ultimately, the businesses failed and our clients were left with huge amounts of debt.

As you think about your earning potential and do your research to identify your best options, you will probably conclude that starting your own business is a risky path to take and may not be the best way to maximize your future earning potential.

If you've done charity or volunteer work, don't dismiss those efforts. Use that experience to enhance your resume. If you aren't working and haven't been a volunteer, get involved with a community group or charitable organization; you will help your community, develop new skills and establish contacts. For example, help coordinate a fundraising event for a charity that you support. Having a successful event will prove you have good organizational, marketing and communication skills, and you will meet and work with new people in the process. These skills and accomplishments will help shape your resume.

There are work-from-home jobs available through the Internet where you could become a "virtual assistant," professional "blogger," service rep, or online teacher. However, before you make a commitment, understand the earning potential as well as the training costs and operating expenses you would incur. It's also a good idea to do a background check on the Internet business using the Better Business Bureau website: **bbb.org**, to make sure it is a legitimate, reputable company.

> *DANGER:* **There are many advertisements on job search websites, through emails and in the newspaper for "secret shoppers" or for at-home jobs promising great hourly rates.** *Many of these jobs are scams. The Federal Trade Commission has information on this topic at their website:* **FTC.gov.** *Don't assume that you will be able to earn the advertised amount of money over an extended period of time.*

Starting a new career with little job experience will probably require additional education or licensing. If this is your desired course of action, list the jobs or careers that interest you. Research the education cost options (loans, grants, online study) and the time factor involved. While you are still married, take classes that will move you closer to your goal. As you formulate a plan to become financially self-sufficient in case there are problems with your marriage, consider that you may have custody of the children. In addition to the education costs, factor in the additional expenses, such as commuting and childcare costs, that you're likely to have if you're working full-time. It is remarkable how many of our female clients tell us they work full-time, but after we discuss the commuting and childcare costs, they are shocked to discover they're barely breaking even. Obviously, calculating employment income and expense options in advance, and giving yourself time to research and prepare while you are still married, will allow you to create a better career plan and put you more in control of your financial future whether you remain married or not.

Analyzing your future earning capability and studying various employment possibilities is an exercise for *your* benefit to increase your financial awareness and long-term survival. In discussing your potential earning power as it relates to alimony or asset distribution, be conservative in your income estimations and use figures that are as realistic as possible. You may conclude that your earning power in the near term will be significantly less than your husband's. With the research to prove this, you will be more effective in requesting a reasonable amount of alimony and/or a more favorable asset distribution. If you are younger with prior work experience and are capable of having a long career with additional education and training, you may be eligible to receive "rehabilitative alimony." This would give you increased alimony support for the period of time that you are training to reenter the workforce until you are able to realize your earning potential.

*In the following chart, write down your job possibilities, any related costs and their estimated potential monthly income:*

## JOB OPTIONS

| Job | Rate/ Hour | Training Cost | Other Costs | Net Income/ Month |
|-----|-----|-----|-----|-----|
| F/T | | | | |
| F/T | | | | |
| P/T | | | | |
| P/T | | | | |
| SELF-EMPLOYED: | | | | |

*Antoinette's Experience:* **After my marriage ended, I was lost. I had worked for many years with my husband in our business, but I had no college education. I studied hypnosis and set up a private practice out of my home, but it didn't produce enough income. Then I took some psychology classes but realized that by the time I graduated with a degree it would be time to retire. I spent four years trying to figure out what I was qualified to do to support myself, and in the process lost all of that time and earning power. Every job I interviewed for, I was either over-qualified or under-educated and my computer skills weren't up-to-date. I eventually got a job, but the point is, divorce, illness or death of a spouse can shove you into the workplace without notice.** *Be prepared, have emergency savings and keep your skills current.*

# DISCOVER YOUR NET WORTH

We have helped you partially answer the question, "*What am I worth?*" by giving you the means to calculate your earning power. The second part of this answer involves finding the value of your net worth: the total value of your assets, minus your total liabilities. Why is net worth important? It tells you the value of what you own, the physical or monetary property you have personally or share in a marriage, measured against what you owe as an individual and as a couple.

Now, it is time to bring out all of the financial folders you created earlier. (The tax return folder can be kept off to the side.) These four folders contain account information for the following:

| | |
|---|---|
| ***"Monetary Assets":*** | e.g., checking, savings, CD's |
| ***"Investment Assets":*** | e.g., mutual funds, retirement accounts, annuities |
| ***"Tangible Assets":*** | e.g., property deeds, vehicle titles, fine arts |
| ***"Debts/Liabilities":*** | e.g., mortgages, student loans, credit cards |

The values in these folders are important for you to know in general because they are partly yours. They are also important when you are trying to get a loan, or if you and your husband were to split up, trying to design a settlement agreement. For example, you and your husband may own a million-dollar home- a highly-valued asset- which might make you feel very wealthy, but if you have a $900,000 mortgage against it, the net asset value you actually share is approximately $100,000. (This asset value does not factor in the costs of selling the home, e.g., agent commission, attorney fees.) Your net worth is a value that you need to ***understand***, to provide the foundation for where you really ***stand*** financially.

The total value of your non-property assets will be found in your monthly or quarterly account statements. Take the first folder's "**Monetary Assets**" account statements and combine them with the statements or financial documents in the "**Investment Assets**" folder. The values for these accounts should be taken from approximately the same time period. Since most statements are provided at the end of each quarter or at year-end, try to pick a recent date, e.g., June $30^{th}$ or December $31^{st}$, when you received statements for everything.

In the following chart, list your most current individual and joint checking account balances, savings accounts, and all investment, annuity and retirement

21

account values. These numbers represent your ***monetary*** or ***liquid*** assets which can easily be converted to cash, and your ***investment*** or ***capital*** assets which provide monetary benefits either through income or increased value.

# MONETARY & INVESTMENT ASSETS

**(Mark each item either J for joint or
I for individual)**

| ACCOUNTS | BALANCE | J/I | DATE |
|---|---|---|---|
| Checking | | | |
| Checking | | | |
| Saving | | | |
| Special Saving | | | |
| CD's | | | |
| Brokerage Account | | | |
| Mutual Funds | | | |
| Savings Bonds | | | |
| Bond Certificates | | | |
| IRA/401k | | | |
| Education Savings | | | |
| Whole Life Equity | | | |
| Other | | | |
| **TOTAL** | | | |

The less liquid assets or property—your "**Tangible Assets**"—include a home, car, trailer, antiques, jewelry, vacation property, time-share, etc. They are items of value but that value is at the mercy of the buyers' market and may take a long time to realize. For example, if you have a trailer that you don't use very often and decide to sell it, you could put an ad in the newspaper or online, but it may take months to get an interested buyer. You can estimate what the value of the trailer should be, but it is very difficult to get that cash value out of it. The trailer is an *illiquid* asset, that is, the monetary value doesn't flow easily from the asset to your wallet. List these property items below using estimated market, appraisal or sale values. The items in these two charts are your total **Assets**.

# PROPERTY OR ILLIQUID ASSETS

**(Mark each item J for joint or
I for individual.)**

| ASSETS | Estimated Value | Ownership | Date |
|---|---|---|---|
| Home | | | |
| Other Property | | | |
| Car | | | |
| Other Vehicles | | | |
| Antiques | | | |
| Jewelry | | | |
| Fine Art | | | |
| Collectibles | | | |
| Other | | | |

Next, determine the value of your debts or liabilities, what kind they are and who is responsible for paying them. Look in the "**Liabilities**" folder and take out the statements. Are they secured or unsecured? Secured debts are attached to a particular piece of property, for instance, a mortgage or car loan. If the loan isn't paid back, the lender can take the property. Unsecured debts are loans that are backed only by your promise to repay them, such as credit card debt. Separate these debt statements into two piles: secured and unsecured. Are your debts joint or individual, installment or revolving? If the debt is individual, then only the account holder is responsible for repaying it. When the debt is joint, either person can be required to pay back the loan; if one person disappears, the other is fully liable. If an account is joint, both of your names will appear in the account title. Make sub-piles of your joint and individual statements under each of the secured or unsecured categories. Installment loans are characterized by a lump sum of money that is initially borrowed, e.g., a fixed-rate mortgage or a car loan, and the payments remain the same each month.

Revolving loans are personal and home equity lines of credit or credit cards. With this type of loan you are given an amount of money or a credit line that is available to you but you don't have to borrow it all at once. When part or all of it is paid back, you can borrow up to the available amount again. The difference between an installment and revolving loan is particularly important, if there are problems in your relationship. With a joint revolving account, like an overdraft line of credit, either person can withdraw whatever is available on that credit line.

The following chart combines the information in the three "**Asset**" folders and the "**Liabilities**" folder. This is also known as a **Balance Sheet**. Anytime you try to get a loan from a financial institution, undoubtedly the lender will ask for your most recent Balance Sheet to determine how risky you are as a potential borrower, given your assets and debt obligations.

On the **Liability** side there are two other categories for debt: short and long-term. The short-term debts can be paid off in one year or less, like medical and credit card debt. Long-term liabilities are debt obligations that are longer than a year like a mortgage, car loan, personal loan or student loan. Place the secured loans which are generally long-term liabilities next to the property they are attached to, with the long-term unsecured debts such as personal and student loans below them. Then list the short-term debts, generally unsecured debts: medical debt, overdraft lines of credit, credit card debt, across from the monetary assets. Place the account owner's initials next to the account name.

# ASSETS & LIABILITIES CHART

| Assets | Value | Liabilities | Value |
|---|---|---|---|
| Checking | | Overdraft Credit Line | |
| Checking | | Medical Debt | |
| Savings | | Credit Card | |
| Money Market | | Credit Card | |
| CD's | | | |
| **Monetary Assets Total** | | **Short-Term Debt Total** | |
| Pension Account | | | |
| IRA/401k | | 401k Loan | |
| Education Acct | | | |
| Investments | | | |
| Mutual Funds | | | |
| Whole Life Equity | | | |
| **Investments Total** | | | |
| Home | | Mortgage | |
| Vacation Property | | Home Equity Loan | |
| Cars | | Car Loan | |
| Other Vehicles | | Other Vehicle Loans | |
| Antiques | | Personal Loan | |
| Jewelry | | Student Loan | |
| Other | | | |
| **Tangible Asset Total** | | **Long-Term Debt Total** | |
| **Total Assets** | | **Total Liabilities** | |
| **Marital Net Worth** | | | |

What do the numbers tell you? If you put all of the assets and debts into one pot, is there any money spilling out or any value left over? Are your assets more valuable than the amount that you owe? If the answer is yes, then part of that value is yours. You have a *positive net worth*.

When you are doing calculations for a divorce settlement agreement, the liquid assets are more desirable and *quantifiable* because they can be turned into cash more easily, so make sure that the distributions are equitable in each category. Many of the clients we counsel agree to divorce settlements drafted by their husbands or husband's attorneys that divide the assets and debts somewhat equally in theoretical value but are unbalanced in terms of liquidity.

> *DANGER*: **Too often, women keep the house for the sake of the children and assume part or all of the mortgage, while the husbands keep their pension, income accounts and part of the credit card debt. Technically the values are similar but women are at a disadvantage because their share of the assets doesn't provide enough cash to pay for the maintenance of the house (mortgage, taxes, insurance, repairs) or cover the basic needs, and they haven't anticipated all of the monthly costs.** *Before signing an agreement, review all of the liquid and illiquid assets and debts, and construct a post-divorce budget. Analyze your housing options and their costs. Consult with an accountant, attorney and financial advisor, if possible.*

If there is a divorce, calculating your worth is only part of the equation that determines what you need or should get financially, but it is an important first step in becoming financially aware and taking control. State laws vary, so you must contact a local attorney to understand your legal rights. Generally, if you have been married for a significant amount of time (ten or more years) and there is a divorce, you are entitled to at least half of the total net asset value acquired during the marriage. Your income or alimony will be a function of you and your husband's earning power and living expense requirements. Any assets you had before the marriage or individual inheritance you received in the interim will usually be kept out of the settlement discussion.

Do you have a better idea of what you are worth? From the previous exercises, calculate an average of your current and future income estimations and the theoretical share of your net asset value in the area below:

## YOUR TOTAL WORTH

| AMOUNT | MARITAL | PERSONAL (est. 1/2) |
|---|---|---|
| Net Liquid Asset Value | | |
| Net Illiquid Asset Value | | |
| Total Net Asset Value | | |
| **TOTAL NET WORTH** | | |
| **MONTHLY INCOME** (estimate) | | |

*(These figures are approximations. Income estimate will include current and potential earnings, alimony and child support. Consult with an attorney and an accountant to fully understand your financial and legal rights, as well as the budget and tax consequences of any divorce agreement. There are websites in the Resources section for legal and financial help.)*

*Antoinette's Experience:* **We were partners in our own business for over 20 years when our marriage ended. Basically our income and lifestyle flowed through the business. When we ended the marriage, we ended the business. I sold our primary home and moved into our vacation house. We split the equity from the home sale and I bought out my ex's share of the vacation house. I assumed the mortgage but had no job and no alimony because he was also out of a job. I did have my retirement account, my half of the money from the home and the business assets we sold. Although there was a small nest egg for the future, I had to professionally reinvent myself in order to get a job so I could afford to pay the bills until retirement.** *If you are in business together and your relationship ends, think about your future living expenses and ask for the amount of income you will need, while you are in the process of negotiating a settlement.*

# YOUR MARITAL BUDGET

We have looked at your overall marital worth, that is, your present and future earning power plus your net worth. The next exercise will focus on your budget and *monthly cash flow* to highlight how you are managing your money at present. It will compare your net monthly income (after taxes and deductions) with your expenses, and show whether your household income is covering these expenses. We will help you chart your monthly income, itemize your monthly spending, and try to make your budget work better for you.

## Current Monthly Income:

We have identified your individual, marital income and possible future income. In terms of your current income, how often does your money come in each month and who has control over where it goes? For simplicity's sake, we will start by assuming that you have full access to the household income and that the earnings or paychecks get deposited once or twice per month. The other income that doesn't come in every month (investment, tax refund) can be pro-rated per month and included in the total, as we calculated earlier in the Average Monthly Household Income Chart.

**CAUTION: If you get a tax refund every year, you are essentially giving Uncle Sam an interest-free loan for 12 months. To avoid giving the government this loan, adjust your payroll exemptions or use a W-5 form to apply for Earned Income Credit if you qualify. By doing so, you can re-channel some of that money into your monthly paychecks.**

Take the Total Combined Income figure from the *Monthly Household Income Chart* and place it at the top of the following Monthly Budget chart.

## Monthly Cash Outflow:

Now, let's list the *essential* expenses for you and your family. These should include what you are currently paying for shelter (mortgage or rent), utilities, transportation, food, clothing, insurance, and medication.

Start with the highest priority expenses, your home and car, since you need a roof over your head and a way to get to work or to the grocery store. If you have a mortgage and car loan, these are secured loan payments that have to be made regularly to ensure you keep possession of your car or home. Some of your other important expenses, such as home or car insurance, might not come in a monthly bill, but you need to account for them in your monthly budget by pro-rating the cost. Then when the bill comes every six months, you have the money set aside to pay it.

Food, lights, heat, and phone are also basic expenses. Fill out the budget chart by referring to your loan and utility company statements, checking account records and credit card statements from the last several months, to estimate what you have recently been paying per category each month. If you haven't been paying the bills and don't have access to past statements, start keeping track from now on. Open the bills as they come in and create a monthly budget going forward.

## CURRENT MONTHLY BUDGET

| AFTER-TAX HOUSEHOLD INCOME: | AMOUNT: |
|---|---|
| **ESSENTIAL EXPENSES:** | |
| Rent/Mortgage | |
| Home Equity Loan | |
| Home Insurance (per month) | |
| Car Insurance (per month) | |
| Car Loan | |
| Property Taxes (per month) | |
| Electric, Gas | |
| Phone, Cell | |
| Internet, Cable | |
| Food | |
| Other Transportation | |
| Medical/Prescriptions | |
| Clothes/Toiletries | |
| Water/Sewer/Garbage | |
| **ESSENTIALS TOTAL:** | |
| | |
| **BALANCE:** | |

What is left over after paying for the basics? We haven't yet looked at unexpected expenses, unsecured debt, miscellaneous items, or savings. If you aren't paying close attention to your expenses, or you and your husband are not coordinating your spending, your budget probably isn't working well.

Refer to your *"Liabilities"* folder to add up the amounts you pay per month on all of your unsecured loans: student loans, personal loans, lines of credit, credit cards, and medical bills. Gather the individual and joint unsecured loan statements from the last few months. Student and personal loan amounts won't fluctuate, but lines of credit and credit card balances and their monthly payments will change. Look at the average monthly balances. Hopefully you are paying off the credit line and credit cards within a month or two, but if you are paying only the minimum, put that amount into the budget.

## MONTHLY BUDGET (Continued)

| PREVIOUS BALANCE: | AMOUNT: |
|---|---|
| **UNSECURED DEBT:** (minimum monthly payment) | |
| Credit Card | |
| Credit Card | |
| Personal Loan | |
| Student Loan | |
| Medical Debt | |
| Store Charge (Credit) Card | |
| **SUB-BALANCE:** | |

Now what is left? Anything? After paying these bills there should be money left to cover miscellaneous items and to put into emergency savings. Look over your checking and credit card statements and write down all of the expenses that would fall under the heading of *"miscellaneous."* These could include gym membership dues, school lunches for the kids, fast food, travel expenses, cigarettes, birthday gifts, magazine subscriptions, dry cleaning, beers, entertainment, etc. Also add in the pocket cash you spend every week on small incidentals like coffee, kid's allowance, and donations. "*Miscellaneous*" can be a huge, money-sucking, black hole of a category, but fortunately it is one where you can exercise some control. Insert a grand total for miscellaneous expenses and see where you stand.

## MONTHLY BUDGET (Continued)

| SUB-BALANCE: | AMOUNT: |
|---|---|
| **MISCELLANEOUS: (examples)** | |
| Entertainment | |
| Dining Out | |
| Dry Cleaning | |
| School Lunches | |
| Gym Membership | |
| Cigarettes | |
| Haircuts/Manicures | |
| Vet Bills | |
| Magazine Subscriptions | |
| Birthday Gifts | |
| Travel | |
| Vacations | |
| Other | |
| Other | |
| | |
| **NET BALANCE:** | |

Is there a positive balance now? Have you been using credit cards as an additional income source, forgetting that it's debt? As counselors, we often find that it is not necessarily the lack of income that causes a budget problem, but the lack of tracking and an uncontrolled amount of spending.

Ideally, after all of these bills are paid, money should be put into a regular savings account for emergencies. There are always unexpected expenses: car repairs, root canals, plumbing problems. And finally there should be a little money left over to contribute to a special purpose savings or investment account for bigger, long-term goal items (e.g., retirement, children's education, vacation). Remember, adding to a savings account, assuming your debts aren't increasing, will result in a higher **Net Worth**.

Many of our female clients complain that most of their income is in the form of an allowance from their husbands, which isn't adequately covering their essential expenses. The husband may be paying for the mortgage, taxes, insurance, utilities and car loans, and giving his wife, our client, a monthly amount of money that he feels is appropriate to pay for everything else. This usually includes food, gasoline, prescriptions, childcare and miscellaneous items.

There are two problems with this method.

The first is a **lack of efficient budgeting**. Neither person is working with the other to produce the best use of the household income. There *is no* household budget. The husband is paying his bills and probably keeping some extra spending money for his own "miscellaneous items" while the wife is trying to finance her portion of the expenses, inevitably funding any shortfall by using credit cards. If they were both working together and evaluating their overall budget needs relative to the household income, adjustments could be made and expenses lowered where necessary.

The second problem is the **lack of financial communication**. There *is no* discussion; the husband makes the financial decisions and the wife feels financially powerless whether she is or not. If she resorts to using her credit cards to pay for part of her spending, inevitably the cards become "maxed out." She has no more credit availability and can no longer use the cards to cover her expenses. In addition, she probably can't afford to pay the minimum monthly card payments, which have been growing steadily with the balances. The wife is embarrassed and afraid to tell her husband about the debt, meanwhile, the husband is using his credit cards for personal miscellaneous expenses which the wife can't calculate or control.

> *DANGER*: **When neither partner communicates, the household budget can get way out of whack while the debt is ballooning. If something happens to the marriage, the wife may be held responsible for all of her credit card debt even though the cards were used for household or children "maintenance" purposes. The increased debt will also affect the marital net worth and consequently the wife's asset distribution in a divorce.** *To avoid this situation, both partners must discuss the overall household budget and live within it. This may be difficult, but if you can get the information together by reading the monthly invoices, including the bills for the mortgage, utilities, insurance, etc., that your husband is paying, and chart the overall budget expenses, it may make more economic sense to your husband to cooperate and coordinate spending.*

The bottom line is that in order to be financially responsible you have to take financial control, realize your individual and marital worth, be aware of your spending and plan ahead. Ideally, once you have tracked the household budget, you should sit down with your husband, go over the *math,* express your concerns, and find financial solutions together. In some cases we have found that the husband actually welcomes a financial dialogue with his wife because he is struggling to handle the budget problems on his own and is reluctant to ask for help.

With the budget figures listed previously, you can more clearly understand the flow of your cash and the extent of your current spending. Does this information give an accurate representation of your real financial needs going forward?

On the next page is a chart for your complete **Marital Budget** or **Cash-Flow Statement**. Put all of the above calculations together in this chart to see the whole picture. Then, in the next section, we will identify problem spending areas, suggest ways to correct them and help you construct a **Revised Budget**. The revised figures will later be filled in alongside the original **Marital Budget** numbers to show how the **Revised Budget** will be more manageable and save you money.

# MONTHLY BUDGET

## MARITAL BUDGET

Date_____

## REVISED BUDGET

Date_____

| Expenses: | Monthly | Expenses: | Monthly |
|---|---|---|---|
| Mortgage/Rent | | Mortgage | |
| $2^{nd}$ Mtg/Home Equity Loan | | New Mortgage (option) | |
| Lot Rent/Assoc. Fee | | Rent (option) | |
| Property Taxes | | Property Taxes | |
| Electric/Gas | | Electric/Gas | |
| Water/Sewer/Trash | | Water/Sewer/Trash | |
| Telephone/Cell | | Telephone/Cell | |
| Internet/Cable | | Internet/Cable | |
| Car Loan/Lease | | Car Loan/Lease | |
| Gasoline | | Gasoline | |
| Parking/ Tolls | | Parking/ Tolls | |
| Public Trans. | | Public Trans. | |
| Car Repair/Fees | | Car Repair/Fees | |
| Home Insurance | | Home/Renters Ins | |
| Car Insurance | | Car Insurance | |
| Medical Insurance | | Medical Insurance | |
| Life Insurance | | Life Insurance | |
| Dental/Eye Care | | Dental/Eye Care | |
| Prescriptions | | Prescriptions | |
| Groceries | | Groceries | |

| | | | |
|---|---|---|---|
| School Lunches | | School Lunches | |
| Childcare | | Childcare | |
| School Tuition | | School Tuition | |
| Student Loan | | Student Loan | |
| Income Tax | | Income Tax | |
| Entertainment | | Entertainment | |
| Sport Fees/Dues | | Sport Fees/Dues | |
| Rec Vehicle Loan | | Rec Vehicle Loan | |
| Pet Expenses | | Pet Expenses | |
| Donations | | Donations | |
| Personal Loan | | Personal Loan | |
| Overdraft Line | | Overdraft Line | |
| Credit Card | | Credit Card | |
| Credit Card | | Credit card | |
| Credit Card | | Credit Card | |
| Vacation/per mo. | | Vacation/per mo. | |
| Gifts | | Gifts | |
| Miscellaneous | | Miscellaneous | |
| Miscellaneous | | Miscellaneous | |
| | | | |
| **TOTAL EXPENSES** | | **TOTAL EXPENSES** | |

| INCOME: | | INCOME: | |
|---|---|---|---|
| Take-Home Pay | | Take-Home Pay | |
| Part-Time Pay | | Part-Time Pay | |
| Child Support | | Child Support | |
| Alimony | | Alimony | |
| Social Security | | Social Security | |
| Rental Income | | Rental Income | |
| Investment | | Investment | |
| Tax Refund | | Tax Refund | |
| Bonus | | Bonus | |
| Other Income | | Other Income | |
| | | | |
| **TOTAL INCOME** | | **TOTAL INCOME** | |
| **TOTAL EXPENSES** | | **TOTAL EXPENSES** | |
| | | | |
| **AVAILABLE SAVINGS** | | **AVAILABLE SAVINGS** | |

# PART II

# Women Empowering Themselves: Financially Surviving Separation

*"When you put your hand in a flowing stream, you touch the last that has gone before and the first of what is still to come."*
*Leonardo da Vinci*

# II

# Women Empowering Themselves: Financially Surviving Separation

## RECALCULATE THE BUDGET

We just laid out your **Marital Budget** and it probably contained a few surprises. If there are problems between you and your husband that may lead to a separation or divorce, you need to become financially proactive by tracking your spending and evaluating your living expense options while you are still married. How much money would you need to support yourself and your children? It is extremely important to keep weekly records of what you spend and put money into a savings account on a weekly basis, no matter how small. Your emergency savings will be your safety net.

The goal is to find out how your expenses can be trimmed, changed or eliminated to give you more financial control over your budget. To successfully seize control, you will need to distinguish between needs and wants. First, you must be able to provide for your basic needs, then make a plan to save for what you want. You will put together a monthly **Revised Budget** to view against the **Marital Budget** and see how the new budget can be more cost efficient, cover all of your needs and provide savings.

The first expense that should be closely evaluated is your housing cost. On average, 30-40% of most budget expense goes toward the rent or mortgage. Taxes, insurance, lawn care, association fees, and repair costs can add 30% on top of the mortgage payment to the cost of maintaining your home.

> *DANGER*: **Your housing options should be weighed before any separation is initiated so the real costs of each option can be calculated. One option may be a loan modification to make your monthly mortgage payments more affordable, but don't forget about the other costs (taxes, insurance) of staying in your home. A loan modification may enable you to stay current on your mortgage but real estate taxes also have to be paid on time. If you get behind on the tax payments, even if you are paying your mortgage on time, you could lose your house in a tax sale.** *Contact your local tax office to work out a modified payment plan if you are having difficulties.*

Mathematically evaluate all of your possible living options first. Calculate the total cost of living in your home and then, as a comparison, research what it would cost to rent a comparable house or apartment in your area, or buy a lower cost home in a nearby area. Include the probable differences in utility costs. You have five possible living options:

1. Staying in your current house
2. Moving and renting a house
3. Moving and renting an apartment
4. Moving and buying a different house
5. Moving in with a family member or friend

## HOUSING OPTIONS

| OPTION | 1 | 2 | 3 | 4 | 5 |
|---|---|---|---|---|---|
|  |  |  |  |  |  |
| Mortgage |  |  |  |  |  |
| Rent |  |  |  |  |  |
| Taxes |  |  |  |  |  |
| Insurance |  |  |  |  |  |
| Lawncare |  |  |  |  |  |
| Assoc. Fees |  |  |  |  |  |
| Maintenance |  |  |  |  |  |
| Utilities |  |  |  |  |  |
| TOTAL COST |  |  |  |  |  |

While trying to weigh these options, you need to consider the amount of equity value in your current house. Look back at your **Asset and Liability Chart** - your **Balance Sheet** - in **Part I** to see if your house value exceeds your mortgage balance.

44

**HOME VALUE** _____ -

**MORTGAGE BALANCE/HOME EQUITY LOAN** _____ =

**HOME EQUITY VALUE: + - (Circle One)** _____

If there is equity value in your marital home, theoretically you could sell the current house and put some of your portion of that equity money into a savings or a retirement account, or you could use part of your equity proceeds to make a down payment on a smaller house. If there is no equity or negative equity, meaning you and your husband owe more on the mortgage than you could get from selling the house, both of you need to discuss and investigate your options.

First, speak to your mortgage lender about the possibility of a refinance or loan modification if your interest rates are high or your monthly payments are more than you can handle. Generally, a refinance will make sense if the current interest rate is more than 2 percentage points lower than the rate you have now, because there are fees and costs involved in redoing the loan. With a loan modification, your monthly mortgage payments may be lowered enough to become affordable. If a refinance isn't a good solution and lower payments can't be arranged or don't result in enough cost savings, a short sale may be an option if the realtor can find a buyer close to your asking price and the bank or lender will accept less than the full amount owed on the mortgage. For further assistance, contact a nonprofit credit counseling agency that participates in the national HOPE NOW Alliance or in local housing initiatives to act as your intermediary. Mortgage assistance sites are listed in the **Resources** section.

After studying the housing options, you may find that the numbers indicate you should sell your home. Your financial survival outweighs whatever sentimental attachments you or your children might have to the house. Of course, it would be nice if you could stay in your home to keep the children in a familiar environment, but not if doing so would result in financial hardship and high stress levels that would negatively affect you all. Unfortunately, selling your house may take time; you may have to live there in the interim and negotiate a housing agreement with your husband to help you manage the living expenses until the house is sold.

Making the right housing choice requires you to separate your emotions from the math, *before* a divorce agreement is finalized. It's a hard thing to do when you're struggling through the separation, feeling guilty and distraught, but your financial survival depends on making good financial decisions. Because your housing cost is a large percentage of your budget, it can make or break your financial plan.

Start the **Revised Budget** using the most economically favorable housing option if your current house can be sold, or with the housing terms that you have negotiated. Then go over your other expenses line by line to see where there are excesses and how they could be lowered.

Below is a chart to identify problem areas in your **Marital Budget** and find solutions. Add other areas that you feel need attention:

| BUDGET PROBLEMS | POSSIBLE SOLUTIONS |
|---|---|
| Adjustable Rate Mortgage (Example) | Loan Modification |
| Multiple Student Loans | Consolidation Program |
| Large Food Expense | Menu-Planning, Coupons |
| Too Many Credit Cards | Credit Counseling Debt Management Program |
|  |  |
|  |  |
|  |  |
|  |  |
|  |  |
|  |  |

# LOWER EXPENSES

There are major expenses and basic monthly expenses. Both types can be lowered by advanced planning, comparison shopping, and identifying the best deals. Major purchases have two cost considerations: their selling price and their monthly cost if financing or a loan is involved.

Let's look at **major purchases** first:

## Home Purchase:

Adults beginning their careers usually start living on their own by renting an apartment. As their income improves and they get married or enter into a relationship, their space requirement grows and they consider buying a home. Frequently, the amount of their rent becomes a baseline housing cost for evaluating an affordable monthly home mortgage payment. This comparison isn't really accurate because buying a house doesn't just involve a mortgage expense, as discussed above. But a home is also an investment. If you can find the right house, in the right location, at the right price, hopefully its value will increase over time and will add to your asset value and net worth. The purchase price is very important, but because most people cannot afford to pay the total cost of a house in cash, they acquire a mortgage or debt in the process of buying it. Therefore, the total purchase price in relation to the total mortgage, plus the monthly mortgage, tax and insurance payments have to be considered as a whole.

In today's lending environment, a home buyer should have enough money saved to make a 20% down payment and have a good credit score to qualify for a loan (more on that topic later). If interest rates are low, which they are now, a fixed-interest rate, 15- or 30-year mortgage, will probably be a better financing option than a variable rate mortgage, since interest rates are more likely to rise over the next 5–10 years. **Bankrate.com** has a mortgage calculator that enables you to figure out how much a monthly payment would be, assuming a total mortgage amount, which will give you an idea of what home price you can afford.

Buying a home is one of the biggest purchases you will ever make. Location and quality of the house are very important; comparison shopping and good pricing are essential; and accurately calculating your total monthly cost—mortgage, taxes, insurance, renovations, repairs—is critical.

## Car Expense:

Purchasing a car through a loan or leasing a car creates a major monthly expense. Maintaining a car results in a basic monthly expense. When you are shopping for a new or used car and plan to finance most of the cost of it, always negotiate the price of the car first, not the monthly loan payments. You want to be sure you are buying the car at the lowest price. Monthly loan payments can be manipulated depending on the interest rate and the loan period. Shop around at various dealers and check the website: **kbb.com**. Kelley Blue Book's site gives new and used prices and trade-in values that many auto professionals use. Don't be afraid to negotiate the price. The best time to purchase a car is at the end of the year when new models are about to arrive and at the end of the month when salesmen are trying to reach their sales quotas.

Keep in mind that if you buy a new car, once it is driven out the dealership driveway, it will probably lose 10–20% of its value, and after a year will lose between 20–40% of its value.[2] So if you take out a car loan, you will most likely be "upside down" in short order, meaning the car will be worth less than the loan outstanding. Consider cars that have the highest resale values to minimize this loss. As an alternative to purchasing a new car, look into buying a slightly used one year old car that still has most of its warranty. Leasing a car may be more practical if you drive less than 12,000 miles per year, but be advised that a lease can contain high fees and early termination penalties, so make sure you review the lease agreement carefully before signing.

In any case, the monthly car payment must be seriously considered in light of your overall budget constraints. Before you go to the car dealer, find out what other lenders, such as banks and credit unions, are offering for car loan rates. Then you can also negotiate with the dealer on the terms of the loan. Car expense not only involves the loan payment but also insurance, license and registration fees, fuel and repair costs. Certain car models will have higher insurance premiums, and some models are more fuel efficient and have lower repair costs than others.

If something happens and you can no longer afford your car payments, giving the car back to the dealer or doing a "voluntary repossession" won't eliminate your obligation to pay the balance of the loan or lease. Once you give it back, the dealership can sell the car at auction and if the difference between what they get and what you owe is negative, what is called a "deficiency balance," you will be responsible for paying that difference. It used to be commonplace to do a trade-in for a lower-priced model if your car payment became too much to handle, but in the current economic climate, car dealers are not inclined to accommodate you.

## Furniture and Appliances:

Comparison shopping is the key to finding the best deal for appliances and furniture, and again, don't be afraid to negotiate. If you are offered a 0% loan to purchase these items, make sure you have the ability in your budget to pay off the loan during the promotional period, before a high interest rate kicks in. Be mindful of the difference between your needs and wants, and know what your budget can handle.

## College Expense:

College tuition can be a huge expense, but there are many ways to get a good education and help with the cost, if you plan ahead. Private schools have expensive tuitions but they usually have a large pool of grant and scholarship money to aid students of merit. Public universities generally have much lower tuitions, particularly for in-state students. A community college (for two-year Associate programs) can be even more affordable and often has ties with a four-year college, so a good student can easily move from one to the other after finishing the two-year program. There are government loans available, and Coverdell and 529 education savings accounts that are savings vehicles with tax advantages. Anyone trying to get a federal student loan or college grant must first complete and submit a Free Application for Federal Student Aid (FAFSA) to be eligible. Many local community and charitable organizations also offer scholarships. The key to evaluating your college expense is to start saving early; work with the high school guidance department to research a variety of schools; identify all possible financial

51

aid sources; and, if necessary, have your child take responsibility for part or all of the student loan. In picking the right college, the total tuition cost is not as important as the net cost to you after all of the financial aid, grants and scholarships are included.

## Vacations:

A vacation is obviously not a tangible thing, but it can be expensive. It is also not an essential expense; it is a want, not a need. The cost of a vacation must closely match what you are able to afford after your basic expenses are paid. Vacation planning should start far in advance. Setting up a special purpose "vacation savings account" and making monthly contributions, even small ones, will help you reach your goal and allow you to pay for most of it in cash, not on credit. Make a list of desirable destinations and do lots of research. There are many online sites that offer attractive package deals, but realize that vacation spending involves more than just the airfare and hotel expense. There will be dining costs, airport parking fees, cab fares, entertainment, gifts, etc. You can use a credit card to charge most of your vacation expenses, but choose a total vacation cost that you can pay off in a month or two, otherwise you will be paying high interest rates on your credit card balances, which will make the cost of the trip much higher and throw your budget off balance.

Now let's look at the **basic expenses**:

## Insurance:

It is important to define the purpose of your insurance and not carry more than you need. Insurance companies are becoming more competitive, particularly for basic home, car and life insurance coverage. Look online for comparable plan rates- **bankrate.com** is a good source. Many of our clients are combining home and car insurance to get a cheaper package deal. Changing your yearly deductible amount, the initial cost that you have to pay out-of-pocket before the insurance policy goes into effect, can lower the premium. For example, if you have a good driving record with no accident claims and currently have a $250 deductible on your car insurance, it might make sense to increase your deductible to $500, which would lower your monthly premium. Depending upon your age, health and family dependent situation, you may want to compare the advantages and disadvantages of "whole life" versus "term" life insurance. If you are in your 30's with young children, term insurance may be more appropriate. Generally term insurance is less expensive, but it has a time limit and no investment component. You should review your insurance needs yearly and make adjustments if there are employment, health or lifestyle changes or your children get older and are no longer dependents.

## Communications:

Many of our clients are getting rid of their land lines and only using their cell phones. They are paring down cable service packages in light of computer video capabilities. Some of the highly advertised "3-Pack" plans (phone, Internet, cable) are actually more costly than the basic plans if you cut out a few deluxe features and more closely estimate your average minute, text message and long-distance usage. Look into combining phone plans with extended family members for additional discounts, and share movie subscriptions and Internet service with neighbors and friends to lower your monthly cost.

## Food:

The food bill is an expense that you can partially control. It can be lowered if you shop once per week, and bring a specific list of items needed for preparing a planned seven-day menu. Healthy meals can be created cheaply from scratch using low-cost ingredients. You can make a big pot of soup from leftovers or stew from less expensive meat or chicken and vegetables in season. Portions of both can be frozen and used for lunches or dinners. The cost can be as low as $1.00-2.00 per serving. Eggs are cheaper than meat and can provide the base for a nutritious breakfast, lunch or dinner. The **Resources** section has good websites and recipes to help you develop low-cost, nutritious meals. Many large grocery store chains have websites with special offers or double-coupon deals that can be used with their regular coupons. The local Sunday newspapers are usually half-filled with coupon offers. If you have food in the fridge but don't know what to do with it, go to **Allrecipes.com** or **FoodNetwork.com** to find dishes that can be made with your ingredients. The **Resources** section also has coupon and money-saver sites.

When you go to the store, buy only what's on your shopping list, don't bring the children, and don't go when you're hungry! If you belong to a large wholesale club, be careful when buying items in bulk. Make sure you look at the "cost per unit" to know how much you're really saving. Sometimes it is actually cheaper at the major chains to buy in smaller amounts. All of this cost-saving effort takes time and organization, but these exercises can make a big difference. Food can be the third-largest expense in your budget.

## Medical costs:

To save on medicine, you can order a 90-day supply of some prescription medications at a discount by mail or online. You can also find a variety of low-cost prescription plans at major drug store chains. Wal-Mart and Target offer some generic drugs for $4 per month. Several wholesale clubs offer discounts on prescriptions even for non-members. If you ask your doctor to prescribe the generic medications that are on your insurance plan list, you can save quite a bit each month. When you can't find a generic substitute, check online retailers such as **drugstore.com** where you may be able to save up to 25%. Only buy from sites that have the VIPPS logo (Verified Internet Pharmacy Practice Sites). Don't buy from foreign online retailers because their ingredients can be different and other countries don't have the same regulation or oversight that we do in the U.S.

Many times manufacturers have different strength medication dosages for about the same price, so you may be able to get a larger dosage and split the pill in half for significant savings. Check with your doctor before you start splitting pills on your own. Pill splitters can be bought online for as little as $2.00. For over-the-counter drug and beauty products, large drug store chains generally have cheaper prices than the major food chains. Some medications that required a prescription in the past can now be bought over-the-counter, for example, Zyrtec.

It is a good idea to review your medications with your doctor and pharmacist annually to make sure you're taking what you need and to check that there aren't better, cheaper alternatives. For dental work, some of our clients go to dental schools where basic procedures can be done at a large discount.

## Miscellaneous:

Finally, tackle the big job of organizing and downsizing your miscellaneous spending. If you or your husband (or kids!) buy coffee, lunch or snacks several times per week, the costs can quickly add up. Buying a sandwich costs about $5.00, while making your own and bringing it from home costs $1.00-$2.00. Cigarettes at $6.00 per pack will cost $180.00 per month for a one pack-a-day smoker. If you eat dinner out twice per week at $40.00 each, cutting down to once a week will save $160.00 per month. As an alternative, have a pot luck dinner and invite your friends. If you have young children who are growing out of their clothes every six months, check out consignment or thrift shops for bargains that are barely worn. Organize swap meets with friends who are the same size or who have children the same age and trade clothes. Household items, small pieces of furniture, dishes, pots, etc., can be found slightly used at **Craigslist.org** or **Freecycle.com** and purchased at bargain prices. If a friend or family member is moving, find out what they're leaving behind or throwing away. Check out **meetup.com** or **flicker.com/groups** where you can join swap groups and trade unused items for desired ones. Instead of going out to the movies, rent a movie and make popcorn at home for big savings. For other entertainment, check out local free concerts, lectures and special events. Haircuts and manicures can be scheduled less frequently and done for half-price at local cosmetology schools.

## You get the idea.

Once you have worked on these budget items and hopefully found ways to spend less, revise your expected monthly costs and put the new figures into the **Revised Budget.** What is the difference between the two budgets? How much income would you *really* need to pay for the basic expenses, assuming a controlled amount of miscellaneous and a regular savings plan? Hopefully, the **Revised Budget** will help you immediately save money and show what you will need to survive on your own. In addition, this exercise will enable you to make more educated decisions about how the marital assets and income should be divided, and how a divorce agreement should be structured.

# TAKE FINANCIAL CONTROL

It's important to know what you're worth and how to budget. To be on a sound financial footing, it is also important to establish your own, ***individual*** relationship with a bank if you don't have one already. While you are still married, you should set up your own checking and savings account (in your name only). The process will be easier if you already have a joint account because the bank will evaluate you based on your marital income and give you preference as an existing customer. Banks offer many types of checking and savings accounts depending on your purpose and time frame, so compare fees, interest rates, and restrictions to find the best product. Again, **bankrate.com** will give you information on the highest industry rates.

Sit down with a bank representative to discuss the options that will best fit your needs and goals. You will become more aware of the products and more in control of your financial future. With tighter control over your budget and a regular savings program, you can begin to build an emergency fund. Even if your husband or boyfriend handles most of the money or pays most of the bills, it's a good idea to have your own accounts and funds, just in case.

*Imagine that the two of you are on a pleasure cruise in the middle of the ocean; he goes off to play golf, you decide to take salsa lessons, and the boat starts to sink. There would have to be two life support systems for you both to survive. Similarly, you need to be the captain of your own financial ship, informed and prepared for the worst, to ensure your own **personal financial survival**.*

*DANGER*: **You can use a joint account to pay for household expenses while you are married, but understand that each of you has the ability to withdraw whatever money is in that account. Therefore, you also need to have an individual checking account. Many times we have had clients whose boyfriends or husbands drained all the money from their "joint" accounts just before announcing an end to the relationship. If the checking account has an overdraft line of credit, he could also tap into the overdraft line and leave you stuck with the debt.** *Pay attention to the monthly activity on your joint account and don't put all of your money into that account. Do not agree to a large joint overdraft credit line.*

We can't emphasize enough the need to review your monthly bank statements to be aware of the money coming in and the money going out of your accounts, individually and jointly. Match the monthly individual and joint bank statements against your budget estimates and checkbook register. If you do banking or bill paying transactions online, keep an expense register of that activity as well and review your budget monthly to understand how much you are spending, where to make adjustments, and how much you can save. For any bank or financial account information or mailing that you want to keep private, open a post office box and have the information sent there.

# MANAGE YOUR DEBT

Whenever you are extended credit or take out a loan (including co-signing a loan with someone else), you are borrowing money and are responsible for paying it back. As we stated earlier, there are two basic types of loans: a secured loan, which is attached to property, and an unsecured loan, which is backed only by your written agreement to pay it. Many married couples jointly own their home and cars and are also jointly responsible for the mortgage and car loans. This is the highest priority debt because if it isn't paid, the lender has the authority to take back the property.

> *DANGER:* **When you co-sign for any loan, secured or unsecured, you will be responsible for paying back the loan if the other person fails to make the payments. Many clients co-sign for their children's car or student loans and end up holding the bag.** *Resist the temptation.*

In the case of credit cards, there can be individual or joint accounts and an authorized user on either of these accounts. The authorized user is allowed to have a card and use it up to the limit, but is not responsible for paying back the debt. Only the owner of the account is legally responsible.

As we already mentioned, when you are tracking and controlling your budget, you and your husband's credit card use has to be closely monitored, particularly if you have joint cards or your husband is an authorized user on your account.

Ideally, credit cards are a convenient way to make purchases. They should not be viewed as an extra money source, even if there is a low introductory interest rate. Zero percent promotional rates may seem like free money, but these offers usually expire after six months and then you can be charged over 20% in a heartbeat. If you are budgeting and responsible with your money, you should spend what you can afford. When you buy an item with a credit card, you are taking advantage of "the float," meaning you don't have to pay for it for a few weeks, so you still have the earning power of your money while the credit card company covers the initial purchase. However, you should buy an item on credit only if you can pay off the balance of the credit card in full by the end of the month. Paying only a minimum monthly payment will trigger an interest charge and extend the principal or loan repayment over a long period of time (as long as 25 years). This can be very costly.

Whenever you apply for or get credit, it appears on your credit report. There are three major credit bureaus: Experian, Equifax, and Transunion. Your credit report contains basic identification information, public records (like crimes, judgments), collection items (old unpaid debt), and your current outstanding debt. The report shows how well you have handled the amount of debt you owe (both individual and joint), whether you are near or over your credit limit, (Are you "maxed out" on your credit cards?), your monthly payment history, the different types of debt you have and how often you have applied for more credit. All of these factors are evaluated based on the Fair Isaac Corporation rating system, resulting in a FICO score, a measure of your credit risk. This score can range from 350 (horrible) to 850 (perfect). It will determine whether you will get approved for a loan and what interest rate you will be charged. Your monthly payment history and credit availability are the two most important components of your score. So, if you manage your debt well, make regular monthly payments, and pay down the balances quickly, you are less risky in the eyes of the lenders, you will have a good FICO score and will qualify for a lower interest rate loan.

Opening your statements each month is a very important discipline for several reasons. The first is to make sure there isn't any unauthorized activity. You have 60 days after receiving your statement to report fraudulent or inaccurate account activity to the credit card company and you won't have any liability if their fraud department investigation backs up your claim. Make sure you follow up any conversation with a letter and keep a copy for your files.

> *DANGER*: **Recently, the credit card companies have become more strict about their definition of "fraudulent." If your husband or boyfriend is not an authorized user but has access to your cards because you keep your wallet or purse in plain sight on top of your bedroom dresser, he could use your card or order something over the phone with your card information. It would be very hard for you to prove that this use was "unauthorized," and you would be responsible for the charge. *Keep your credit cards and wallet in a safe place at all times. Do not give out your bank or credit card account information to anyone who isn't an owner or authorized user.***

Secondly, you want to know that *your* charges are being reported accurately and if an authorized person uses the card, you want to know what they have charged, since *you* are ultimately responsible if they don't pay. Thirdly, you need to read each monthly statement to understand the rates and terms of the card. The credit card companies have the ability to change your interest rates and credit limits without notifying you. (When you first get a card, there is a disclosure statement listing all of the card company's lending terms in microscopic lettering.) If they *raise* your credit limit, it's usually a good indicator that you have been responsible, making your payments each month and paying down the balances in a reasonable amount of time. A good payment history helps your credit score and generally results in an increase in the amount of credit available to you, which also helps your credit score.

Credit card companies also have the ability to *lower* your credit limit without calling or telling you, so if you think you have a $2,000 limit on your card and you have charged $1,000 on it, you may assume that there's still $1,000 left to spend. However, if the credit card company sees that you acquired and charged on a few new credit cards or have been a day or two late paying one of them, they could lower your limit to $1,500. Then if you charge $600 more without realizing the change, you are suddenly over the limit, hit with an over-the-limit fee and charged a higher interest rate. Calling and yelling at the representative will do you no good and may result in your card being closed. Tracking your monthly spending and reviewing your monthly statements will keep you informed and help you stay in control.

Everyone is allowed to get their credit report for free from each of the three main credit bureaus, once per year. You can get your credit report through the mail or online at **annualcreditreport.com**. It is incredibly important to know what is on your report. If you have a joint account with your husband or boyfriend, or he is an authorized user and you are having problems in your relationship, you want to be aware of your account activity and liability. On the report, under the type of debt, there will be an "I" meaning "individual", a "C" meaning "contractual" or J for "joint" (both signify co-ownership), and "A" meaning "authorized" to describe the owner of the debt. Some clients don't know what debt they are responsible for or if they are simply authorized users. Your report will tell you.

Be aware that identity theft is the fastest-growing crime in the country.

> *DANGER*: **Dumpster-diving is a booming industry! If you throw away any of your financial statements with the garbage, thieves can hunt through the trash and take anything that gives them even part of your account information, putting you deeply in debt and creating a credit nightmare if you are unaware.** *Get a paper shredder, if possible, or cut up your personal papers and place them in a garbage bag with watery food scraps so the paper and ink will be destroyed.*

Cut up your old cards that haven't been used recently but may still be open, and shred any account statements before throwing them out. Immediately report fraudulent activity to the credit card company and credit bureau by phone and *in writing,* and make a copy of all correspondence for your files.

Keep track of your report every few months and you will spot any illegal or unauthorized activity. Credit reports can have errors on them that could negatively affect your score. A recent study determined that 80% of all credit reports have some type of an error. We counseled one client with an unusual name, something like "Sylvester Bartholomew," who was trying to get a loan but was rejected because of his bad credit score. He thought his score should have been stellar but when he got his report, saw that many of the debts and delinquencies weren't his. He later found out there were two other "Sylvester Bartholomews" living in his town and their debts and credit profiles had been mixed in with his. It took our client over two years to untangle the debt and remove the errors. In the meantime he couldn't get approval for any loan.

When you are looking for a job or think you may need to apply for a job in the near future, know that today over 70% of employers will pull your credit report before hiring you. They must get your permission, but often when you fill out an employment application there is small print under the signature line stating that when you sign the application you are authorizing them to pull your report. The reasoning is, if you are irresponsible with your debt, you will probably be an irresponsible employee, and if you have a large amount of debt, you will be more likely to steal from the employer. It is a good idea to pull your credit report a few months before you start job hunting, knowing that the employers will be reading it. This will give you time to resolve any errors or disputes.

At the Federal Trade Commission website: **FTC.gov**, you can download and print dispute forms that should be filled out and sent to the credit bureaus along with proof of errors, ownership, loan payoffs, fraudulent activity, etc. Keep copies of all correspondence. Do not call a representative to try to fix any problems—credit card companies and the credit bureaus have hundreds of call-center employees. You will never speak to the same person twice or get the original person back on the phone. Do all of your disputes and dealings with the credit bureau in writing. Once you send a dispute form asking for verification that a particular debt is yours, the credit bureau is required to send you written evidence within 30 days of receiving the inquiry, otherwise the debt has to be wiped off your report.

If you are interviewing with a potential employer and know that there are inaccuracies or disputed items on your report, you can explain that you're in the process of resolving the errors. This will show the employer that you *are* responsible with your debt even if your credit report implies otherwise. More information on credit reports and disputes is provided in the **Resources** section.

Getting behind on credit card payments can have serious consequences with respect to your credit report, but also understand that if you get totally overwhelmed and decide not to pay on the cards—not pay back the loans—the consequences can be disastrous. After a few months of non-payment, the credit card companies may take a look at your current and potential income and assets and decide to take you to court to get a judgment against you. This judgment, an official court ruling, gives the card company the right to attach a lien to one of your assets or garnish part of your present or *future* wages. If you are having debt problems, don't try to run away from them; you can't hide forever. Whatever you owe while you're hiding will continue to accrue interest and late fees, increasing the balance at a rapid rate.

> *DANGER*: **Credit repair companies advertise that they will fix your credit for a few hundred dollars. These companies are simply writing to the credit bureaus every 30 days, asking for written verification of your debts. If the credit bureau doesn't respond in time, by law, these debts have to be removed from your report. Trying to remove these debts is all that the companies are doing to "repair" your credit. *This is something you can do yourself, for free. You can send the dispute form to the credit bureaus requesting verification of any or all of your loans.***

Instead, call the credit card company to ask about enrolling in their internal "hardship program" where the interest rate is reduced, or contact a nonprofit credit counseling agency to help you find a solution. There is a chart provided on the next page where you can list each card you have, your balance owed, minimum monthly payment and A.P.R. or Annual Percentage Rate of interest that you are currently paying. When you call the credit card companies, ask for the best internal program that they are willing to give you, the interest rate, minimum payment and length of time until the debt is paid, then add that information to the chart.

Be aware that the credit card company may offer to enroll you in an internal program in exchange for closing your card. They may automatically close your card just because you asked about the program or about lowering your interest rate. No matter what, don't agree to enroll in a program unless you know that your budget can handle making the required program payments every month. If you agree and can't keep up with the payments under their program, the credit card company will kick you out and not allow you to enroll in any other debt management program for years.

Be wary of any "credit relief" or counseling agency that advertises it can eliminate most of your debt. Trying to get rid of your debt this way can have serious tax consequences and trash your credit report. Whenever there is a notation on your report that you have settled a debt for "less than full balance," it signifies that you have not paid what you owed, similar to a bankruptcy. If you have $10,000 worth of credit card debt and the credit relief company gets the creditor to settle for half of the balance or $5,000, the IRS considers the $5,000 that you are "forgiven" as income and you will have to pay income taxes on it. Negative (and positive) information on your credit report will be shown for seven years, unless it is disputed and found inaccurate (and except for certain bankruptcy cases, which stay on the report for ten years).

Speak to a ***nonprofit*** credit counseling agency to get counseling advice and find out what their **debt management program (DMP)** would do for you. After a counseling session, if the counselor feels the program is the right solution, the agency will send you the debt management program paperwork with your specific budget, approximate debt program interest and monthly payment figures. Nothing is official or binding until you sign and return the paperwork. Write down the agency program information next to the credit card company internal program information you have compiled, to get a clear picture of your choices compared to what you are paying now.

## CREDIT CARDS

| CARD NAME | Balance | Interest Rate | Monthly Payment | Internal % Rate | Internal Payment | DMP % Rate | DMP Payment |
|---|---|---|---|---|---|---|---|
| | | | | | | | |
| | | | | | | | |
| | | | | | | | |
| | | | | | | | |
| | | | | | | | |
| | | | | | | | |
| | | | | | | | |
| | | | | | | | |
| | | | | | | | |
| MONTHLY TOTAL | | | | | | | |

*CAUTION*: **Even though student loans are unsecured, if they are through a government agency or federal program, these loans will stay with you forever, even in bankruptcy. Do not ignore them and think they will go away because the agency hasn't sent you a notice.** *You must pay back student loans. The student loan agencies will work with you in most cases if you communicate with them and explain any financial difficulties you're having. They will offer hardship programs to help people who qualify.*

# BUILD GOOD CREDIT

Having bad credit history is a problem, but so is having no credit history. If you are just starting out in the work force or living on your own, building good credit takes planning and effort. Getting a store charge card is usually easier than getting a major credit card, and the limit is relatively low. Making a small purchase (something you need) with the card and paying it back over one or two months will start a payment history. It is very important to pay on time, which means getting the payment in the mail or scheduled online several days prior to the due date. If you make a few purchases over six months and pay them off promptly, you will undoubtedly start getting major credit card offers in the mail at "low promotional" interest rates.

These offers are not the same as free money—read the fine print. Getting a major credit card is very useful, but if you accept one of the promotional deals, make sure you review your budget and understand how you can make the card work for you; charge for necessities such as gasoline or groceries and pay off the balance each month. ***Remember, using a credit card is taking out a LOAN.***

If you are not able to get a credit card, another way to begin a credit history is to get a secured credit card through your bank. You put a certain amount of money into a savings account and the bank will issue you a card that is "secured" or backed by the funds in that account. For example, if you put $250 into the account, you will be able to charge up to that amount, minus any fees,(which can be high so check that out before you apply). Make sure that the bank reports this card's payment history to the credit bureaus (not all secured cards are reported). After approximately six months of good behavior with this card, major card offers should start to appear. That doesn't mean that you should apply for them all, because doing so would hurt your credit score. Review the credit card agreements, promotions and rewards, and pick one major card.

Revising your budget, improving your spending habits, and controlling your debt will give you more power over your financial future. You must give yourself a financial check up each month and update your files and financial statements regularly. At this point in your life, there are three words that you need to repeat: ***save, save, save.***

# PART III

# Financially Alone: Women Empowering Themselves

*"Power can be taken but not given. The process of the taking is empowerment itself."*
*Gloria Steinem*

# III

# Financially Alone: Women Empowering Themselves

## UNTANGLE JOINT DEBT

The process of divorce is tortuous. Dealing with bills, lawyers, accountants and an estranged husband, and at the same time managing the household, children, and everyday activities requires almost super-human strength and serious mental control. Sorting out the income, assets and debt can be mind-numbing, but having the budget information and financial statements at hand will help the process.

A separate checking and savings account provides a crucial safety net to protect you during this period. If you are well informed about your budget, you should be able to move quickly into a survival mode if necessary and cover your basic costs until you can generate enough income and the divorce agreement is finalized.

You need good legal advice. Get referrals from friends and interview several lawyers. Retainers and hourly rates will vary and so will personalities. Find an attorney who will fight for your rights, work *with* you and *for* you. In many states, once an attorney meets with you, he or she is precluded from representing your husband in the divorce, to ensure the confidentiality of the information you shared during the consultation. That rule can work in your favor if you interview the best local attorneys before your husband does, or against you if he acts first. Go to **findlaw.com** for a list of lawyers in your area if you don't have any referrals. Do a background check by calling your state's Bar Association to make sure there are no complaints against the attorney before you hire him or her. If you cannot afford a good lawyer, contact your local Social Services Office and speak to someone from Legal Aid or go to **lawhelp.org** for assistance information. Understanding the laws of your state, and being financially proactive and prepared as soon as possible, will allow you to design the best financial settlement agreement concerning your marital assets and debts, alimony and child support.

> *DANGER*: **Your divorce agreement may state that your husband must pay for half of the mortgage or take over half of the credit card debt. However, the mortgage lenders, banks or credit card companies won't automatically remove you from the obligation.** *Some loan accounts, if joint, may have to be closed and new individual ones opened, to make sure the liabilities are correctly transferred.*

Let us reiterate: *focus on the math*. Your future is at stake. Don't agree to anything until you understand your rights and options. The divorce process can take anywhere from several months to several years. You previously calculated your earning power and net worth. Don't sell yourself short during the negotiations just to "get it over with." Take out all of your financial records, review your **Revised Budget, Balance Sheet** and re-evaluate your worth. If you and your husband have partnership interests or investment properties, get the most current documentation that indicates their approximate value. If there are retirement savings, depending on the type, the annual contribution may show up on your IRS tax return, but also be aware of what and where the retirement accounts are, and what other potential compensation or bonuses might be forthcoming that don't appear on the returns. Find out what you need to do in your state to obtain a Qualified Domestic Relations Order (QDRO), a court order that you give to your husband's retirement plan sponsor to prevent your husband from making withdrawals from any retirement account during the divorce process.

Be diligent about keeping copies of both your and your husband's monthly account statements throughout this period. These statements include those concerning your assets: e.g., checking, savings, and investment accounts, as well as loan and credit card statements. You don't want any surprises such as disappearing assets, nor do you want to have ballooning debt. There is a worksheet in the **Appendix** where you can list all of your joint and individual account information: the exact name of the account, institution, account number, address and phone number.

> *DANGER*: **Sometimes a husband's bank, investment or partnership accounts can suddenly "disappear" at the onset of divorce discussions and end up "off-shore" in some tropical island bank deposit box.** *If you haven't done prior research and don't have records of these accounts in your file, you may have to hire a forensic accountant to search for your husband's financial assets, which can be time-consuming and very expensive.*

Having monthly files containing account information as reference and proof will definitely speed the process along and make it less likely that some assets will be transferred or more debts incurred.

When you are drafting a divorce agreement, insurance coverage and retirement assets need to be thoroughly discussed. If you have been covered by your husband's medical insurance plan, the law states that you must be offered continued coverage through a COBRA (Consolidated Omnibus Budget Reconciliation Act) plan for up to 36 months after the divorce. Whether he continues to pay for the coverage or you pay monthly should be spelled out in the divorce agreement. Life insurance policies, such as whole-life plans and annuities, can also be investment and retirement vehicles with asset value. Make sure you address all of the insurance policies and accounts and divide their equity values as part of your agreement. Amend life insurance coverage, if necessary, to satisfy the divorce agreement stipulations and to cover your husband's financial responsibility to you and your children in the future, in case something happens to him.

*Hollis' Experience:* **When my husband and I were drafting our divorce agreement, our three daughters were teenagers, close to college age. I was asking for ten years of alimony, and child support. Since I wasn't working and he had the medical policy through his work, he also agreed to pay all medical costs for the girls. In the event that something were to happen to him, he purchased a life insurance policy with me as the beneficiary, which would cover his total responsibility for alimony, child support, and a portion of the college expense.** *If you are relying on your husband for alimony, child support or other income contributions, think ahead and make provisions in your divorce agreement that will anticipate the worst. Make sure he sets up enough life insurance, with you as the beneficiary, to cover his total financial commitments to you and your children.*

Talk to your lawyer about the estate laws before the divorce is finalized. Review your will to make sure your assets will be distributed properly and the beneficiary designations for retirement and life insurance accounts are amended. If you don't have a will, draw one up.

*"The art of war teaches us to rely not on the likelihood of the enemy's not coming, but on our readiness to receive him; not on the chance of his not attacking but rather on the fact that we have made our position unassailable."*
*Sun Tzu* [3]

Think about how you can best become financially independent. You know your husband's financial behavior. If his income or potential earning power is questionable or unsustainable, then your divorce agreement should rely less on his paying you monthly alimony and child support and more on your receipt of a larger portion of the liquid assets or lump sum payments up front. Just because your agreement states he must pay monthly child support or alimony, doesn't mean he will abide by it. If he stops paying, you will probably have to take him to court to fight for the money owed, and that will take time and involve legal fees.

*Hollis' Experience:* **My husband was in his mid-50's during our divorce and had been working in the New York City financial district for over thirty years. I realized his income level probably wasn't going to last much longer, and decided it would be prudent to receive a larger chunk of the marital assets when the divorce became final. As part of our agreement, before the divorce was finalized, we sold the marital house and bought another house in both of our names, using part of the proceeds of the marital house for the down payment. We took out a joint mortgage on the new house since I didn't have the personal income to qualify on my own. As part of the divorce decree, the title of the new house was transferred to me and the mortgage was paid off with a portion of my husband's asset distribution. I had the new house free and clear to live in with my three daughters.** *In exchange for getting a larger percentage of the assets, I agreed to limit the alimony period to ten years, at which time I would be able to start withdrawing money from a retirement account to supplement my income. According to the laws in my state, after twenty years of marriage, I had the right to ask for alimony for the rest of my life.*

80

As the divorce moves through the final stages, keep your emotions in that separate compartment and stay focused on the numbers. How are the assets and liabilities or debts going to be divided? Does this division make sense for your financial needs? Have you been able to get a full-time job? What are you going to be able to earn and what can your husband afford to pay in alimony and child support every month? Using the previous **Asset and Liabilities** chart as a reference on the next page, list the assets and liabilities that will be assigned to you after the divorce. Then list all of your expected income sources.

# POST-DIVORCE
# ASSETS & LIABILITIES CHART

## DATE_____

| Assets | Value | Liabilities | Value |
|---|---|---|---|
| Checking | | Personal Loan | |
| Savings | | Medical Debt | |
| CD's | | Line of Credit | |
| Investment Accounts | | Credit Card | |
| Mutual Funds | | Credit Card | |
| Pension Account | | Credit Card | |
| IRA/401k | | 401k Loan | |
| Education Savings Account | | Student Loan | |
| Whole Life Insurance | | Policy Loan | |
| House | | Mortgage | |
| Vacation Property | | Home Equity Loan | |
| Car | | Car Loan | |
| Other Vehicles | | Other Secured Loans | |
| Other Property | | Other Mortgages | |
| Antiques/Fine Art | | | |
| Jewelry | | | |
| Other | | | |
| | | | |
| **Total Assets** | | **Total Liabilities** | |
| **NET WORTH** | | | |

# POST-DIVORCE MONTHLY INCOME

| | |
|---|---|
| Take-Home Pay | |
| Child Support | |
| Alimony | |
| Social Security Benefits | |
| Rental Income | |
| Investment Income | |
| Other Income | |
| **TOTAL INCOME** | |

Do you have a positive net worth and are most of your assets liquid? Will you be able to have savings and investments as a cushion and an additional income source? Will you have to sell assets to supplement your income? Does the **Revised Budget** you created earlier reflect your expected monthly income and expenses?

Assuming you are not keeping your marital home, you have already reviewed housing costs and have an idea of what your best housing option would be. Check **realtor.com** for up-to-date housing and rental prices if you need to move. Once you have found a reasonable house or apartment to rent, adjusted your budget, and put enough into emergency savings, you can start thinking about short- and long-term goals.

*CAUTION*: **After the divorce, the woman is usually the main caregiver for her children and family. When her children are grown and there are grandchildren, she frequently assumes the primary responsibility and cost for family gatherings and holiday celebrations. This role can cause food and miscellaneous costs to increase dramatically.** *Anticipate your role as the family's social center and include these extra expenses in your alimony calculation.*

On the following page construct your **Post-Divorce Budget.** Enter your total income figure below the expenses to determine the positive or negative balance:

# POST-DIVORCE BUDGET

| EXPENSES PER MONTH: | AMOUNT: |
|---|---|
| Mortgage/Rent | |
| Lot Rent/Association Fee | |
| Property Taxes | |
| Electric/Gas | |
| Water/Sewer/Garbage | |
| Telephone/Cell | |
| Internet/Cable | |
| Car Loan/Lease | |
| Gasoline | |
| Parking/Tolls | |
| Public Transportation | |
| Car Repairs/Fees | |
| Home/ Renters Insurance | |
| Car Insurance | |
| Medical insurance | |
| Life Insurance | |
| Dental/Eye Care | |
| Prescriptions | |
| Groceries | |
| School Lunches | |
| Alimony Payment | |
| Childcare/Daycare | |
| School Tuition | |

| | |
|---|---|
| Student Loan | |
| Income Tax Payments | |
| Entertainment/Dining Out | |
| Donations | |
| Sport/Gym/Dues/Fees | |
| Pet Expenses | |
| Boat/Rec Vehicle Loan | |
| Personal Loan/ Line of Credit | |
| Credit Card Payment | |
| Credit Card Payment | |
| Credit Card Payment | |
| Vacations (pro-rate monthly) | |
| Clothing/Toiletries | |
| Gifts | |
| Smoking | |
| Other | |
| | |
| **TOTAL EXPENSES** | |
| | |
| **TOTAL INCOME** | |
| **TOTAL EXPENSES** | |
| **BALANCE** | |

If you do not have positive net worth, no assets to utilize or invest, and your budget is barely balancing, remember you have the most control over food and miscellaneous spending. There are also good resource programs to assist with food, utility costs, children's medical coverage, phone plans, etc. Most states have set up a general resource assistance hotline number: **211** (a 3-digit phone number just like 911 for emergencies). You can also go online to **211.org** to find out what programs are available in your area that you may qualify for. Assistance sites are also listed in the **Resources** section.

# SET YOUR GOALS

You are now wearing the captain's hat onboard your financial ship, but it will take time to get your bearings and plot your course. Hopefully you are getting all of the stipulated payments from your ex, bringing home your own paycheck and living within the confines of your revised budget. This budget will be a work in progress, needing constant attention and adjustment.

Have you thought about any short- or long-term financial goals? What would you like your money or assets to do for you?

Make a list of your financial priorities:

| SHORT-TERM GOALS | TIME | LONG-TERM GOALS | TIME |
|---|---|---|---|
| **Vacation (sample)** | **Summer 2009`** | **Retire in Florida** | **20 years** |
| | | | |
| | | | |
| | | | |
| | | | |
| | | | |

Most short-term financial goals can be achieved through the use of special-purpose savings accounts. Generally, it's better to separate regular savings from special savings because you're less likely to tap into your special savings account if an unexpected expense occurs. You can have several special savings accounts if you want, one for each short-term goal. In the case of planning for a vacation, do the research, then come up with a target vacation savings amount. Review your overall budget and savings ability, holding back some money for emergency savings. If the vacation you choose will cost $2,000 and you want to go away in 10 months, you'll need to save an extra $200 per month or $50 per week. Is that doable? Maybe the time frame will need to be stretched out longer. If you keep track of your income and spending every month, and know what amount of savings is possible, then you can construct a plan, follow your course, and have that vacation.

Generally, our clients' two most important long-term goals are saving for their children's college education and having enough money for a comfortable retirement. The best way to achieve these goals is to take advantage of tax-deferred savings vehicles. However, it is important to realize there are many ways to pay for college and your children can take over some or all of that financial responsibility. They can apply for grants and student loans, do work-study programs or enroll in a community college for the first two years, then transfer to a four-year college to get their undergraduate degree.

*Antoinette's Experience:* **My three sons were working in the family business when our marriage broke up and the business partnership ended. I had co-signed for my sons' student loans, but the loan payments were being deducted from their salary. When the boys found other jobs, they moved on. The business had paid off the two older boys' loans, but the last child still owed $90,000 on his student loan; the business couldn't pay it; and it was still in my name. I have been paying for college tuition since I got married and never went to college myself. I paid my husband's student loan and now I'm left with the student loan for my third child.** *Do not sign or co-sign for your children's student loans. You can help pay for them if you can afford it. Save money for your retirement first.*

Saving for retirement, on the other hand, is totally your responsibility, so it should be a top priority. Women generally earn less money over their careers and live longer. They also tend to take care of others before considering their own needs. Many of our clients spend a big chunk of their income or get heavily into debt paying for their children's college tuition. Then, as retirement age approaches, they realize there isn't enough money in savings to retire.

According to the Women's Institute for a Secure Retirement (WISER), the five top retirement challenges for women are:

1. Three out of five working women earn less than $30,000 per year.
2. Three out of four working women earn less than $40,000 per year.
3. Half of all women work in traditionally female, relatively low-paying jobs without pensions.
4. Women retirees receive only half the average benefits that men receive.
5. Women's earnings average $.77 for every $1 earned by men, a lifetime loss of over $300,000.

# ACHIEVE YOUR GOALS

If you are in your 30's, 40's or even 50's, your primary financial concern should be putting money into a retirement account every year for the tax advantages and the compounding value. The following table shows the effects of putting $200 per month into an IRA starting at age 30, and what you would sacrifice if you wait to contribute.

# RETIREMENT SAVINGS CHART: (4)

The sooner you begin saving, the greater your future savings balance. For example, if you wait just one year to start your savings plan, you will have $37,709 less at retirement than if you started saving today. The table below illustrates how postponing your savings plan would impact future value.

### Savings and Assumptions:

| | | |
|---|---|---|
| Current age | 30 | |
| Anticipated retirement age | 65 | |
| Annual savings amount | $2400 | |
| Annual saving increases: | (%) | 0% |
| Before-tax return on savings: | (%) | 8% |
| Marginal tax bracket: | (%) | 20% |
| Compounding/savings frequency | 12 | |

### Future Value of Retirement Savings

| Years To Wait | Start Age | Years To Accumulate | Yearly Amount | Future Value At Retirement (before-tax) | Future Value At Retirement (after-tax) |
|---|---|---|---|---|---|
| 0 | 30 | 35 | $2,400 | $461,835 | $314,327 |
| 1 | 31 | 34 | 2,400 | 424,127 | 292,560 |
| 2 | 32 | 33 | 2,400 | 389,308 | 272,138 |
| 3 | 33 | 32 | 2,400 | 357,157 | 252,979 |
| 4 | 34 | 31 | 2,400 | 327,471 | 235,005 |
| 5 | 35 | 30 | 2,400 | 300,059 | 218,142 |
| 6 | 36 | 29 | 2,400 | 274,749 | 202,322 |
| 7 | 37 | 28 | 2,400 | 251,378 | 187,480 |
| 8 | 38 | 27 | 2,400 | 229,798 | 173,556 |
| 9 | 39 | 26 | 2,400 | 209,872 | 160,493 |
| 10 | 40 | 25 | 2,400 | 191,473 | 148,237 |

The earlier you can start investing for retirement the better. Many women lack the confidence to initiate an investment or financial retirement strategy, mainly because they don't have the financial knowledge or the discretionary income. The investment universe is huge and complex, with new products coming out every year. We won't attempt to give an adequate explanation of the pros and cons of different investments in this small guide. But if you have assets that you would like to invest for retirement or college tuition, or want to open personal investment accounts, we recommend working with a professional financial advisor. Similar to the way in which you interviewed your legal representative, you need to take time to research and interview several different investment advisors. Check into the background of the advisor and the brokerage or advisory firm through FINRA (Financial Industry Regulatory Authority) at **finra.org/brokercheck** to make sure there aren't any suits or complaints against them.

Your financial advisor should be primarily interested in helping you achieve your goals, not in selling you the latest product with the highest commission. A good advisor will meet with you and get to know you, to understand your values, concerns and financial needs. Then, together you can come up with a suitable plan. He or she should advise you and guide you through the process of formulating an overall investment strategy considering your age, priorities and risk tolerance.

Once you have set up a retirement savings plan, if there is additional money available, you can open an education savings account for your child. The websites: **pathtoinvesting.com** and **wiserwomen.org** provide good, clear information on retirement, investment and education accounts. There are other good websites that can familiarize you with basic investment terms and concepts while you are working with a professional. These sites are listed in the **Resources** section. Don't be afraid to ask as many questions as you need to understand your options, the costs and the risks involved.

When your budget has been finely tuned and the savings, investment and retirement vehicles are in place to steer you toward your goals of financial independence and security, you can take a deep breath and pat yourself on the back. Not only have you survived, but you have learned how to manage your budget and personal finances. The fourth power source—money—is working for you to fuel your success. You are now acting like the captain of your financial ship, empowered with the ability to control your financial destiny. It feels good, doesn't it?

# PART IV

# Financial Tools for Women Empowering Themselves

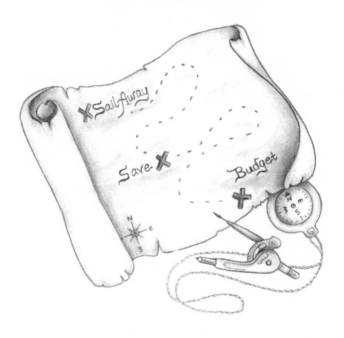

*"Tools are only powerful when in use."*

# IV

# Financial Tools for Women Empowering Themselves

## RESOURCES

**Employment Assistance:**

www.Rileyguide.com - network and support info for jobs

www.Job-hunt.org - job search support groups, employment services

www.Execunet.com - networking and career management services plus professionals available for advice, support

www.40Plus-non-profit.org. - executive employment help site

www.bpwusa.org - Business and Professional Women networking and help site

## Legal:

www.abanet.org - American Bar Association Family Law
    Section

www.acresolution.org - Association for Conflict
    Resolution - mediators

www.afccnet.org - Association of Family and Conciliation
    Courts

www.Findlaw.com – listing of local attorneys by category

www.Lawhelp.org – legal assistance and information

www.nolo.com – legal information and education site


## Living Assistance:

www.211.org - resource site by state, county
    (phone = 211)

www.AngelFoodMinistries.org – food program
    (not income based)

1-800-21-SHARE – food program, in most areas
    (not income based)

www.aarp.org – information for seniors

www.LIHEAP.org - home energy assistance programs
    (income based)

www.Rxassist.org - database of patient assistance programs

www.drugstore.com – online prescriptions at a discount

www.benefitscheckup.org – programs available for seniors

www.caregiving.org – National Alliance for Caregiving

www.stretcher.com – general budgeting and saving
    help site

www.coupons.com – general coupon site

www.couponcabin.com – general coupon site

www.couponmom.com – general coupon site

www.retailmenot.com – coupon programs from a variety
    of stores

www.smartsource.com – general coupon site

www.craigslist.org – local site for used items,
    job offerings, information

www.flickr.com/groups – swap groups

www.meetup.com – swap groups

## Financial and Consumer Help:
## (alphabetical listing)

www.AmericaSaves.org - general savings tips

www.asec.org - American Savings Education Council

www.bankrate.com - info on bank rates, mortgage rates, credit cards, insurance, taxes, Financial Literacy Series, news, financial advice

www.bbb.org - Better Business Bureau - quality reviews and complaint ratings on businesses

www.CardTrak.com – info on credit cards, secured cards, rates, offers

www.betterinvesting.org – investment, financial education information

www.cpf-board.org - Certified Financial Board of Standards for Financial Planners

www.fafsa.ed.gov – Free Application for Federal Student Aid

www.fanniemae.com - info on approved mortgage lenders and defaulted loans

www.federalreserve.gov - consumer information, financial education

www.FINRA.org - Financial Industry Regulatory Authority for broker and Investment Adviser check

www.401k.org - Profit Sharing/401K Society of America

www.freddiemac.com – info on federal mortgage loans

www.FTC.gov – Federal Trade Commission - basic consumer information site: (partial article list)

Credit Cards and Consumer Loans
Avoiding Credit and Charge card Fraud
Building a Better Credit Report
Co-Signing a Loan
Credit and Divorce
Credit and Your Consumer Rights
Understanding Vehicle Financing
Financial Readiness: In Case of Emergency
Finding a Job:
Work-at-Home Schemes
Federal and Postal Job Scams
Job Scams/Telemarketing Scams
FTC Blogs

finance.yahoo.com -financial markets and personal finance site

888-995-HOPE – Hope Hotline, free foreclosure-prevention services

www.irs.gov – Internal Revenue Service info and past IRS tax returns

www.jumpstart.org - general financial education

www.mint.com - secure online budget tracking system

www.msmoney.org - financial info for women, online tools

www.mymoney.gov - US Government's financial education website www.nfc.org - National Foundation for Credit Counseling

www.pathtoinvesting.org - financial education for students and adults, ABCs of Investing, Financial Self-Defense for Women

www.salliemae.com – student loan info

www.sba.gov – Small Business Administration for loans and resources

www.score.org - info and resources for self-employed from retired professionals

www.smartmoney.com - info, resources, articles on personal finance

www.66ways.org - Consumer Literary Consortium site, advice from experts on how to save on 28 major product areas

www.360financialliteracy.org - American Institute of Certified Public Accountants site, savings and personal finance advice

www.upromise.org- shopping portal for 529 education savings accounts

www.wiseupwomen.org - US Dept of Labor financial site for women

www.wiserwomen.org - retirement and financial education and information in cooperation with the U.S. Administration on Aging

# Appendices

# Appendix I

# Account Information List

**Date_____**

| ACCOUNT | OWNER | ACCT NO. | BALANCE | PHONE |
|---|---|---|---|---|
| Checking & Savings: | | | | |
| | | | | |
| | | | | |
| | | | | |
| Investments: | | | | |
| | | | | |
| | | | | |
| CD's: | | | | |
| | | | | |
| | | | | |
| IRAs/401k: | | | | |
| | | | | |
| | | | | |
| Mortgage: | | | | |
| | | | | |

| ACCOUNT | OWNER | ACCT NO. | BALANCE | PHONE |
|---|---|---|---|---|
| Home Equity Loan: | | | | |
| | | | | |
| Car/Vehicle Loans: | | | | |
| | | | | |
| | | | | |
| Personal Loans: | | | | |
| | | | | |
| | | | | |
| Student Loans: | | | | |
| | | | | |
| | | | | |
| Credit Cards: | | | | |
| | | | | |
| | | | | |
| | | | | |
| | | | | |
| | | | | |
| | | | | |

# Appendix II

# Weekly Miscellaneous Spending Log

**Week of** _____

| ITEM | M | T | W | TH | F | SAT | SUN |
|------|---|---|---|----|---|-----|-----|
|      |   |   |   |    |   |     |     |
|      |   |   |   |    |   |     |     |
|      |   |   |   |    |   |     |     |
|      |   |   |   |    |   |     |     |
|      |   |   |   |    |   |     |     |
|      |   |   |   |    |   |     |     |
|      |   |   |   |    |   |     |     |
|      |   |   |   |    |   |     |     |
|      |   |   |   |    |   |     |     |
|      |   |   |   |    |   |     |     |
|      |   |   |   |    |   |     |     |
|      |   |   |   |    |   |     |     |
|      |   |   |   |    |   |     |     |
|      |   |   |   |    |   |     |     |
|      |   |   |   |    |   |     |     |
|      |   |   |   |    |   |     |     |
|      |   |   |   |    |   |     |     |
|      |   |   |   |    |   |     |     |
| TOTAL |  |   |   |    |   |     |     |

# MISCELLANEOUS SPENDING LOG

## Week of _____

| ITEM | M | T | W | TH | F | SAT | SUN |
|------|---|---|---|----|----|----|-----|
|  |  |  |  |  |  |  |  |
|  |  |  |  |  |  |  |  |
|  |  |  |  |  |  |  |  |
|  |  |  |  |  |  |  |  |
|  |  |  |  |  |  |  |  |
|  |  |  |  |  |  |  |  |
|  |  |  |  |  |  |  |  |
|  |  |  |  |  |  |  |  |
|  |  |  |  |  |  |  |  |
|  |  |  |  |  |  |  |  |
|  |  |  |  |  |  |  |  |
|  |  |  |  |  |  |  |  |
|  |  |  |  |  |  |  |  |
|  |  |  |  |  |  |  |  |
|  |  |  |  |  |  |  |  |
|  |  |  |  |  |  |  |  |
|  |  |  |  |  |  |  |  |
|  |  |  |  |  |  |  |  |
|  |  |  |  |  |  |  |  |
| TOTAL |  |  |  |  |  |  |  |

# MISCELLANEOUS SPENDING LOG

## Week of _____

| ITEM | M | T | W | TH | F | SAT | SUN |
|------|---|---|---|----|----|-----|-----|
|      |   |   |   |    |   |     |     |
|      |   |   |   |    |   |     |     |
|      |   |   |   |    |   |     |     |
|      |   |   |   |    |   |     |     |
|      |   |   |   |    |   |     |     |
|      |   |   |   |    |   |     |     |
|      |   |   |   |    |   |     |     |
|      |   |   |   |    |   |     |     |
|      |   |   |   |    |   |     |     |
|      |   |   |   |    |   |     |     |
|      |   |   |   |    |   |     |     |
|      |   |   |   |    |   |     |     |
|      |   |   |   |    |   |     |     |
|      |   |   |   |    |   |     |     |
|      |   |   |   |    |   |     |     |
|      |   |   |   |    |   |     |     |
|      |   |   |   |    |   |     |     |
|      |   |   |   |    |   |     |     |
| TOTAL |   |   |   |    |   |     |     |

# Appendix III

# Monthly Budget Ledger

## DATE_____

| EXPENSES PER MONTH: | AMOUNT: |
|---|---|
| Mortgage/Rent | |
| Lot Rent/Association Fee | |
| Property Taxes | |
| Electric/Gas | |
| Water/Sewer/Garbage | |
| Telephone/Cell | |
| Internet/Cable | |
| Car Loan/Lease | |
| Gasoline | |
| Parking/Tolls | |
| Public Transportation | |
| Car Repairs/Fees | |
| Home/ Renters Insurance | |
| Car Insurance | |
| Medical insurance | |
| Life Insurance | |
| Dental/Eye care | |
| Prescriptions | |
| Groceries | |
| School Lunches | |

| | |
|---|---|
| Alimony Payment | |
| Childcare/Daycare | |
| School Tuition | |
| Student Loan | |
| Income Tax Payments | |
| Entertainment/Dining Out | |
| Donations | |
| Sport/Gym/Dues/Fees | |
| Pet Expenses | |
| Boat/Rec vehicle Loan | |
| Personal Loan/ Line of Credit | |
| Credit Card Payment | |
| Credit Card Payment | |
| Credit Card Payment | |
| Vacations (pro-rate monthly) | |
| Clothing/Toiletries | |
| Gifts | |
| Smoking | |
| Other | |
| | |
| **TOTAL EXPENSES** | |
| | |
| **TOTAL INCOME** | |
| **TOTAL EXPENSES** | |
| **BALANCE** | |

# Appendix IV

# Menus

*Double up on any of these menus and put some in the freezer for lunch or dinner!*

## PASTA BOLOGNESE:

2 tbs olive oil
2 tbs butter
1 small onion
2 cloves garlic
1 28 oz can crushed tomatos
½ lb chopped beef
½ lb chopped pork
2 lb pasta
¼ lb romano cheese grated

Heat butter and oil in frying pan
Sauté onion, garlic and meat until meat is brown
Add the tomato
Simmer until the sauce thickens (about ½ hr)
Boil pasta according to directions
Drain and pour sauce over pasta
Serve with crusty bread
Serves 5 people at $3.20 per person

## SAUSAGE AND PEPPERS:

2-3 lbs of Italian sweet sausage
4 red, yellow or green peppers (in season)
1 Vidalia onion
Salt and pepper
3 yellow or red potatoes cut into wedges

Bake sausage at 400 degrees for 15 min or until brown
Place remaining ingredients in baking pan and bake additional 20 min
Serve with crusty French or Italian bread
Serves 4-5 people    Cost: $2-3 per serving
Makes great leftover sandwiches.

## CHICKEN SOUP:

1 whole chicken
5 carrots
1 celery stalk
1 large onion
6 bullion cubes and water
Salt and pepper to taste
1 cup flat noodles or small pasta

Place all ingredients in a pot on top of the stove
Cover chicken with water (3-4 quarts)
Cook until chicken falls off of the bone (about 1 1/2 hrs)
Remove chicken from bones and place back in the soup
Boil pasta, drain and add to the soup
Serve with crusty bread
Serves 4-5 people  Cost: $2-3 per serving

# ONE PAN MEAT LOAF DINNER:

2 lbs chopped meat (beef)
3 yellow potatoes cut into wedges
1 white onion chopped
Salt & pepper to taste
2 eggs
1 cup plain bread crumbs
2 cups ketchup
½ box frozen peas

Chop the onion and save half
Mix : meat, half onion, eggs, pepper, salt, bread crumbs,
1 cup ketchup
Mold into a loaf
Place in roasting pan
Surround with potatoes, other half of onion and peas
Cover the meat with the remaining cup of ketchup
Salt and pepper the potatoes
Bake for one hour or until the meat is cooked.
Makes great leftover sandwiches
Serves 4-5 people   Cost: $2-3 per serving

# BAKED HAM:

4 to 5 lb ham with bone
1 cup dark brown sugar
1 can pineapple rings
1 tablespoon mustard
Tooth picks

Place ham in pan
Mix sugar, juice from the pineapple and mustard
Pour over the ham
Garnish ham with pineapple rings (secure with tooth picks)
Bake ham according to directions on the ham or about
1 1/2 hrs
Serve with baked sweet potatoes and green salad

**Great for ham sandwiches the next day!**
**Save the bone for pea soup !**

Total meal cost :          $16-19.00
At ½ lb per person, serves 5 people
Cost: $3.00-$4.00 per person with leftovers for lunch

(Use ham bone in following soup recipe)

# PEA SOUP:

Leftover ham bone
I bag of peas for making soup (located in the soup aisle)
1 onion
3 carrots

Follow directions on the back of the bag
This makes a huge pot of delicious soup
Serve with crusty bread and a basic green salad
Use leftovers for lunch

Cost: Less than $1.00 per person